Series Editor **Mike Burghall**

The MINIMAX Teacher

Minimise teacher input and maximise student output

Jon Taylor

Published by
DELTA PUBLISHING
Quince Cottage
Hoe Lane
Peaslake
Surrey GU5 9SW
England

First published 2001
Reprinted 2004, 2006

ISBN-10: 0-9533098-9-4
ISBN-13: 978-0-9533098-9-4

Designed by Christine Cox
Cover illustration by Phillip Burrows
Project managed by Chris Hartley
Printed by Halstan & Co. Ltd., Amersham, Bucks, England

Acknowledgements
The publishers would like to thank Liz Sharman for her valuable editorial contribution.

This book is dedicated to all teachers great and small.

Contents

Acknowledgements

I would like to thank the following friends and colleagues for their direct or indirect help and encouragement in the writing of this book:

Mari Carmen Aldonondo, Kevin Bachelor, Mike Burghall, Anna Calabrese Bassi, Sarah Bryant, Christine Cox, Jean Paul Crétan, Sheelagh Deller, David Fischer, Arthur Ford, Helena Gomm, Maaike Grit, Chris Hartley, Mary Henley, David A. Hill, Steve Jones, Joan McCormack, Rob McRae, Della Mitchener, Amos Paran, Nicolas Ridley, Mario Rinvolucri, Maria Ruggiero, Debbie Smith, Maggie Smith, Glen Stephen, Shane Swift, Penny Ur, Steve Watts, Ron White, Mark Wilson, Jim Wingate, Su Woodwards.

I am grateful to the following for their ideas for activities:

Mari Carmen Aldonondo (Activity 57), Kevin Bachelor (Activity 13), Jean Paul Crétan (Activities 47, 84, 86), Mary Davis (Activity 85), Sheelagh Deller (Activities 11, 40, 87), David Fischer (Activities 68, 80), Arthur Ford (Activity 63 Variation 3), Mary Henley (Activity 24 Extension), Rob McRae (Activity 1 Variation 1), Amos Paran (Activity 56), Mario Rinvolucri (Activities 27-30, 63), Glen Stephen (Activity 3), Shane Swift (Activity 52), Steve Watts (Activity 48), Ron White (Activity 61), Ken Wilson (Activity 35), Jim Wingate (Activity 26), Su Woodwards (Activity 73).

Bibliography

Appel, J. 1995. *Diary of a Language Teacher.* Oxford: Heinemann.

Carré, C. 1993. The First Year of Teaching. in Bennet, N. and Carré, C. (Eds.) 1993. *Learning to Teach.* London: Routledge.

Chisholm, B., Kearney, D., Knight, G., Little, H., Morris, S. and Tweddle, D. 1986. *Preventive Approaches to Disruption: Developing Teaching Skills.* London: Macmillan Education.

Deller, S. 1990. *Lessons from the Learner.* Harlow: Longman.

Edge, J. 1989. *Mistakes and Correction.* London: Longman.

Gardner, H. 1993. *Frames of Mind: The Theory of Multiple Intelligences.* London: Fontana Press.

Grinder, M. 1991. *Righting the Educational Conveyor Belt.* Portland: Metamorphous Press.

Honey, P. and Mumford, A. 1992. *The Manual of Learning Styles.* Maidenhead: Peter Honey.

Kolb, D. 1976. *The Learning Style Inventory Technical Manual.* Boston: McBer.

Lowes, R. and Target, F. 1998. *Helping Your Students to Learn.* London: Richmond Publishing.

Revell, J. and Norman, S. 1997. *In Your Hands - NLP in ELT.* London: Saffire Press.

Tice, J. 1997. *The Mixed Ability Class.* London: Richmond Publishing.

Underwood, M. 1987. *Effective Class Management.* London: Longman.

Ur, P. 1981. *Grammar Practice Activities.* Cambridge: CUP.

Willis, D. and Willis, J. (Eds.) 1996. *Challenge and Change in Language Teaching.* Oxford: Heinemann.

Willis, J. 1998. Task-based learning. English Teaching *professional.* Issue 9.

Wingate, J. 1996. Multiple Intelligences. English Teaching *professional.* Issue 1.

Wingate, J. 1997. Multiple Intelligences and Lesson Planning. English Teaching *professional.* Issue 2.

Foreword

This book is written in the belief that many teachers feel overworked and under stress, and it attempts to address both issues. What may seem remarkable is that it is possible to reduce both workload and stress *and* do a better job. This is achievable because:

- as teachers, we frequently do a lot of unnecessary work.
- students can take on responsibility for much of that work.
- it is in the students' own interest to do so.
- action at the right moment can save effort and time later on.

The MINIMAX approach aims to increase efficiency by reducing teacher input in the interests of both teacher and student, in such a way that the students learn more effectively by being more involved in their learning. In the extreme, it implies getting the maximum from the minimum.

The MINIMAX approach

All the activities in this book can be used with little or no preparation time and an absolute minimum of materials. It is hoped that you will find them realistic, adaptable and useful at a variety of levels, but also that you will be able to step back and recognise a larger, more complete picture: a genuine 'approach', which is more than simply the sum of the activities proposed.

Many of the activities are not original; while some are still in their original form, others have changed beyond recognition, and many have been springboards for completely new activities. You are recommended to adapt them similarly, to change them or to use them to invent new ones in line with your own teaching style. It is important not to say 'I can't use this activity', but to ask *how* it might be used in your classes.

The MINIMAX teacher

The book explains how you might start off with a new class, but including a MINIMAX approach in your current teaching is straightforward. Some of the activities are probably so similar to your own favourites that your students wouldn't notice the slightest difference. The difference will be felt more by you, and be reflected in the longer term progress of the students.

MINIMAX is not a radical new methodology sweeping aside all that has gone before it; it will fit in with most approaches, from Grammar Translation to Task-Based Learning. But whatever your teaching style, the ideas in this book should make life easier for you, more productive for your students ... and much more fun for you both!

Jon Taylor

Introduction: The Road to Efficiency

I've met the following teachers during my career. Maybe you've met them too. I've given them different names here.

John is conscientious, creative and under stress. Right now he is glued to the staffroom table designing a handout for his next class. On the noticeboard is a sign advertising a seminar on how to cut down preparation, but with four more handouts to do, he's not sure he can afford the time ...

Mary is creating a crossword puzzle for her teenagers. Before her is a list of vocabulary and a complicated diagram, and she's trying to get the words to interlock appropriately. Last time they did the puzzle in five minutes, so she still has the rest of the lesson to plan when she's finished this ...

Jane is learning far more about the English language, and far faster, than her students, even though they pay and she gets paid. Designing worksheets has really helped, even improved her own spelling, though the students barely seem to look at them ...

Adam prepares extra material for the faster students in his mixed-ability class, but it never seems enough. He exhausts himself keeping them occupied, while they get restless waiting for the others, who are trying to catch his attention ...

Jack has made some beautiful flashcards, sticking neatly cut out photos onto card with adhesive film. He's done six but needs 20 for this afternoon, so he's got a long way to go ...

Roy can run off a good handout in record-breaking time, but he bins it after every lesson. Right now he needs one, just like one he made last year. It's a pity he doesn't have it with him now ...

Helen is preparing a role-play debate, writing out instructions on slips of paper, distributing attitudes and opinions evenly amongst the class, clearly telling them what to think. She's forgotten that last time they refused to defend beliefs they didn't hold, it took ages to explain the vocabulary and the whole activity was rather a disaster ...

Sally has got some great games for her classes, especially quizzes. She writes the questions, chooses the teams, explains the rules, asks the questions, gives feedback, keeps the score, controls behaviour and checks for cheating. The students, well, they answer the questions, if they can ...

Pete plans some great lessons and really puts everything into them, but his teenagers find them either too easy or too dull, they rarely get involved and are often disruptive. So the harmonious experience he had in mind frequently becomes a battle of wills ...

Judith has filled her car boot with sets of notebooks to mark. Some exercises require her careful attention and professional judgement, while others could be marked quickly and mechanically. The most frustrating part is giving them back: the students hardly ever look at her comments, they just want their score out of ten ...

Mark can never keep tabs on pieces of paper and cannot lay his hands on record sheets, which is embarrassing in staff and parents' meetings. Students' essays frequently go missing and materials are often out of place ...

The fictitious teachers opposite represent typical situations. Do you recognise them, and to what extent is there a problem?

One common feature of these situations is that the teachers are overloading themselves and underloading the students. Considerable effort is normally required for learning to take place, and the teacher who takes on too much of the burden deprives the students of an integral part of the learning process.

A squash coach is a true MINIMAX artist, taking two steps to send the pupils running all over the court. They wouldn't learn half as much just by watching, so they do most of the work, pay for the lesson and thank the coach.

Minimising input

Preparation can often be creative and satisfying, and as you prepare you often think about your students, their attitudes, needs and progress. But with a busy timetable it is desirable to keep preparation time to a minimum, so you need to build up a collection of activities which require little preparation, like the ones found throughout this book, and involve your students in your lesson design (see Principles 2, 3 and 4 on page 10).

Energy

A great deal of energy is expended in class if we always assume a central role. Putting the students to task and in the spotlight will conserve this energy (see Principle 3 on page 10). Also, energy is frequently wasted trying to tie up those loose ends which should have been firmly bound from the start (see Chapter 1 on the issues of starting off with a class and getting control of activity and behaviour).

Spoken input

We use our voices in class for presenting language samples, modelling, drilling, describing, explaining, exemplifying, eliciting, narrating, reading aloud, giving instructions, controlling activity and monitoring behaviour, correcting, giving feedback and conversing. How can we economise on all of these?

- Some students will know what we are about to present: we can elicit and enrol their help in the presentation and explanation.
- Eliciting can be done silently, by gestures and visual prompts.
- Modelling can also come from cassettes, videos and strong learners.
- Drilling often comes too early, and is therefore wasted. Learners need time for language to sink in before they are forced to repeat it.
- Students can also take part in describing, narrating, reading aloud, etc.
- Correction and feedback are not functions for the teacher only.
- Controlling activity and behaviour are easier in an organised environment.
- Giving instructions is best done in the presence of silence.
- Most teacher-talk can be done at conversation pitch: we must avoid straining our voices.

Maximising output

Oral production

Students should not be forced to produce new language too soon, but with more familiar language the sooner the teacher activates them the better. Teacher-spoken input is an extremely rich resource for the students, but if the teacher dominates the dialogue, inefficiency creeps in. You don't need the practice as much as they do. Passive listeners may become restless and inattentive through lack of involvement. Teachers frequently fill the silences which, in fact, represent thinking space for learners. It is also a strain to keep up entertaining conversation on an hourly, daily basis. But most important, perhaps, is that learning necessarily takes place through trial and error: students need, therefore, plenty of opportunity for such trial.

In a 'question and answer' drill, for example, why can't the students produce both questions and answers as early as possible? If you model *What's your favourite colour?* yourself every time, you deny the students the practice and the discovery of the information themselves. Instead, elicit the question until they can all say it, then activate the practice. Personalisation (see Chapter 2) allows for creative, meaningful substitution drills perfectly, and you don't have to prepare handouts with the answers on; simply allow the class to discover each other's favourite things and report back to you. In the balance between teacher-talk and student-talk it is easy to appreciate that increasing output can be a direct result of reducing input.

Fewer handouts, more language

It is tempting to march into class laden with materials, believing this to be in the students' best interests. But effective language learning lies in challenge, engagement and learner activity, so it would be better if the students marched in laden with materials! Photocopying usually suggests that you want students to read more text than they already have access to, eg. in their coursebooks or at the newsagent's. Even if there is little text, it still involves reading. But if there is little text, why go to the trouble and expense of photocopying, when you can dictate the contents, giving listening and writing practice as well as the opportunity for language analysis (breaking it down) and synthesis (putting it together)?

Photocopiable materials often involve lists, eg. survey questions and debate topics. Why not dictate one item per student, and then ask all the students to mingle and use that language? They will all encounter the whole list, but by listening and speaking, rather than reading and speaking. The former is arguably more enjoyable, too, and will prepare students better for conversation: it will necessitate requests for clarification, negotiation of meaning and repetitions. Think how dry mere reading sounds by comparison! Furthermore, if they all have a different question each, there will be more surprise elements and a realistic reason to listen (see Activities 49 and 50).

With all materials, the challenge for the teacher is to make the printed word come alive, to get students to comment on, copy or say it in a fully engaging activity. Photocopying provides more printed words, but doesn't promise to bring them alive; the teacher still faces the same challenge.

Less mother tongue, more target language

There will be occasions when it is quick, simple, appropriate and accurate to use the students' first language (L1) in class, eg. translation may be the most effective way of explaining an abstract concept, thus saving time and effort. However, there are plenty of reasons to be careful with such an approach: it is inappropriate in a multilingual class; translation can be misleading or inexact; it can breed laziness; it robs the students of chances for real communication. If students are taught English through Italian, for example, they are learning that English is a 'school subject' like any other, while Italian is a medium of communication. This has the danger that as soon as something exciting or worrying crops up, much time is spent (and opportunity lost) discussing it in the mother tongue, rendering the lesson inefficient.

If everything is done in English, the students are exposed not only to the target language of the lesson but to all the natural language of instructions, prompts, explanations, warnings and other exchanges, which are presented in useful, highly frequent and authentic chunks. Students can learn as much from what they notice peripherally as from the focus of the lesson.

Communicating for a purpose

Let us take a specific example of a specific teaching point, and look at the wider implications. You want to check the understanding of *knife*, *saw* and *hammer*. Dialogues A and B are two fictional classroom dialogues which differ in efficiency (T = Teacher; S = Student):

Dialogue A

T: What do you call the tool a carpenter uses to cut wood?
S1: Pardon?
T: What do you call the tool a carpenter uses to cut wood?
S2: What's a carpenter ?
T: It's a person, an occupation. Someone who makes things with wood. So what do you call the tool a carpenter uses to cut wood?
S3: A saw.
T: That's right, well done. Now, what do you call ...

What is happening here? In Dialogue A the teacher gets all the speaking practice and encourages only short contributions from a limited number of students. This is good exposure, but if it goes on throughout the lesson the teacher will be tired and the students quite possibly bored and frustrated, with little sense of progress, achievement or involvement.

Dialogue B

T: What's a hammer?
S1: It's a tool.
T: What kind of tool?
S2: For hitting ... what are they?
S3: Ah, those metal things ...
S1: Yes, in the wall ...
S3: Nail.
S2: That's right, nails.
T: So what's a hammer?
S1: It's a tool ... for hitting nails ... into a wall.

What's the difference in this example? In Dialogue B the questioning is reversed, and the teacher offers much less and elicits the longer definition. The students work together, recycling vocabulary and sometimes teaching each other, in order to produce the answer, which is not just one word, but a useful chunk of language. The students have to do quite a lot of thinking, analysing and synthesising. They are involved and engaged. The teacher has stepped back from the action yet still directs, using gestures and contributions where necessary. In Dialogue A the teacher is making a perfectly acceptable start, which can still be developed by eliciting the question back from the students, and making sure that the answer contains a similar stretch of language.

Here is a third dialogue for the same lesson:

Dialogue C

T: Imagine you have three tools: a knife, a saw and a hammer. Which would you find most useful on a camping holiday?
S1: I don't know, I never go camping!
S2: No, I don't go. But perhaps a hammer?
S3: I think a knife.
S4: What is a knife?
S1: For cutting, you know, in a restaurant, you have knife, fork ...
S2: Ah! You prefer a restaurant to camping!
S4: So a knife is for cutting. But a saw is also ...
S2: Isn't a hammer also useful ... for camping?
S3: Not nowadays - tents don't need ...

In this example the students are given a task which requires as much linguistic precision as in Dialogue B, but language has become the communicative framework serving the achievement of the task. In other words, the language has a purpose. They can teach each other, contribute their own knowledge and also find out about each other. Student 3 may know more about camping than the teacher, in fact the teacher may have chosen this topic for that reason, knowing that S3 doesn't usually speak a lot. Dialogue C therefore includes personalisation (see Chapter 2).

A word of caution

The emphasis of this book is to try to make teacher input more effective, not to do away with preparation altogether. Well-planned lessons are essential if a teacher is to be professional, and every step of a lesson must be principled. It is important to understand the rationale behind the MINIMAX principles and activities before trying them out in the classroom. Cutting down on some aspects of their workload frees teachers for more effective work in class. There is nothing in this book which advocates the wholesale, indiscriminate abdication of authority and responsibility on the part of the teacher.

The MINIMAX Principles

1 Minimise teacher input, maximise student output

Improving efficiency for teachers involves numerous variables and can therefore be achieved in many ways. Inputs such as time, effort and energy can be reduced or saved; outputs such as tangible work from students, language practice and production can be increased, accelerating other outputs such as learning. Redressing the ratio can also cut down on unwanted by-products such as stress, fatigue, burnout and disruption, releasing teachers to reconsider their role and allowing them the time, space and peace of mind to be more effective.

2 Use personalisation and the students' imaginations

Personalisation can provide meaningful content for lessons and frees the teacher from having to prepare materials or fabricate artificial opinions or roles. Students are more likely to enjoy describing their own house, or their ideal house, or even their idol's house, than the one in the coursebook. Parents might feel more at home describing their own children rather than the people in the flashcard you have made. Learners already have opinions on topics relevant to them: they only need linguistic prompting, rather than elaborate roles embracing someone else's views. In these ways they have more control over the content, and there is a real information gap; not even the teacher can correct the factual accuracy. Furthermore, it is realistic practice: things close to the students, like expressing their true feelings, are relevant examples of communication in the real world. If they meet English-speaking people and make friends, these are the things they will talk about. Teachers can also save themselves a great deal of effort by tapping into the students' imaginatons for lesson content. This is more fully explained in Chapter 2.

Students respect being consulted about their course, as it shows that their contribution and their feelings are important and that your course will respond to them. Needs analysis, feedback, self-evaluation and regular counselling are realistic and practical applications of personalisation outside the direct classroom syllabus.

3 Put the focus on the students

Maintaining the focus on you, the teacher, means that you are the centre of attention, and if it happens all the time it assumes that you are the instigator and initiator of activity, the source of knowledge and authority for correction, the judge, timekeeper and scorekeeper, the administrator and organiser, the scribe and machine operator, the caretaker and the monitor of behaviour. This is demanding, and there are stressful moments, eg. meeting a new class, or when students get over-excited during a game, or when you are stuck for ideas on a thorny language query.

The focus can easily be switched from you to the students, even in the first lesson, by setting appropriate tasks. It is in everybody's interest that you do so, as it not only lightens your load, but addresses the problem of attention limits and restlessness, involves the students more and gives them more opportunities to produce language. You may also find you have tighter control over the proceedings from 'a back seat', giving you more time and freedom to assess their language and provide help where needed. Students will enjoy taking on classroom tasks, as this instils responsibility, creates dynamism and relieves tedium. It is the teacher who is often reluctant to relinquish them.

4 Encourage student-generated activities

Frequently, a great deal of language work goes into pre-lesson preparation which would be far more effective as part of the lesson plan. For the teacher it may be an unproductive chore; for the student, valuable practice or revision. As well as being fun, the preparation is probably more effective practice for students than merely completing the answers in an exercise you have designed. Remember, too, that your enjoyment in preparing a new lesson may not transfer across to your class! As well as being motivating and challenging, student-generated activities can be helpful with mixed levels, and in avoiding disruptive tendencies.

5 Keep materials simple, and keep them

Materials do not have to be meticulously prepared. Loose cut-out photos have a number of advantages over mounted laminated cards. For one, they are lighter and less bulky, and therefore more easily carried and stored. Also, they are smaller, so you can fit more onto a table-top. Adding to them is quick and this keeps the collection fresh. If they get torn or lost, they are not difficult to replace and you can be consoled in the knowledge that you didn't spend hours producing them. If you can store your materials efficiently, they will build up to form an effective toolkit for you, but without taking up too much space. All resources, including student-generated materials, can be kept for revision or for use with other classes.

6 Be flexible, and make the most of your preparation

Don't make your lesson plan too rigid; the students may want to steer it in a different direction. They may be enjoying an activity and want more time, or they might like to initiate discussion unexpectedly. In such cases, it is worth capitalising on their interest. Also, some remedial work may require an appropriate diversion. Save the material you have prepared for a later lesson, and save yourself some time in the process.

Flexibility is valuable in activity design, too. Many great ideas can be recycled, extended and adapted for different levels, ages and class sizes. An activity you have used for a grammar point may be suitable for vocabulary or pronunciation areas. Preparation is an investment, so make it work for you.

7 Share correction

To deal with speaking errors, follow the simple pattern of *Perpetrator, Peer, Professional*. When errors occur, as they must for effective development, indicate by means of recognisable gestures that something is wrong, and give the students the chance to correct themselves first. If they need help, turn to the rest of the class. Finally, the teacher can step in to clarify if necessary. This procedure gives everyone more reason to listen, as there's a chance to participate and confirm theories.

Should you correct written work yourself? If a word is mis-spelt, for example, the teacher is not the only class member qualified to rectify it. In time, and with co-operation and practice, trust between learners can be engendered, and they can show their work to each other for feedback. In the process, the learners are reading meaningfully, being exposed to another person's style of writing and possibly new language, keeping an antenna out for mistakes, and learning about writing techniques. It is important for the teacher to monitor the learners' performance during this procedure, of course, but the rewards include the fact that marking the final draft is much quicker and the work is of a higher standard: not only a teacher's dream, but surely a teacher's objective.

8 Organise and share responsibility

Organise yourself, organise your students, and organise your students to help you. The first point is obvious, and the benefits include looking and feeling professional. The second involves setting up routines and making expectations clear. The third answers this question: How much administration and preparation could your learners profitably help you with? This means handing the students some of the responsibility for their learning. What does that mean? Negotiation and Needs Analysis will help you with syllabus design (but keep plenty of surprises up your sleeve to avoid predictability). In pair- and groupwork, students may help each other and, in so doing, reinforce their own knowledge. If they ask each other for help it shows they trust each other's knowledge. Study skills help students become more autonomous by revealing good learning habits, showing that it does not all rest on the shoulders of the teacher.

Allowing students to choose makes them proud of their choices, leading them to take more care over quality. The choice might be which photo to describe, how to tackle a task, what to write about, who to ask the next question, whether to listen with eyes shut or pen in hand, or which homework exercise to do. Organising the classroom, collecting and distributing materials, using and cleaning the board, operating and looking after equipment, keeping track of attendance ... all these are activities which can be shared, to huge educational benefit.

9 Start as you mean to go on

Classroom control has everything to do with efficiency: if you can start well, you save yourself time, energy, patience and stress later, you achieve more, the students are more appreciative, lessons are more enjoyable and you sleep more easily at night. Furthermore, the earlier and the more you can engage your students in activity, the easier it is to avoid wasted energy and negative 'vibrations'. You will never have your class more in the palm of your hand than in the first lesson, so you must seize the opportunity to create the relationship you want.

10 Respect your students as people

- Learners are not empty vessels to be filled with knowledge from the teacher, or a restless, passive audience to be entertained by the teacher.
- Learners come to class with a wealth of knowledge about their world.
- Learners will already know some English before their first lesson, even complete beginners.
- Learners use their existing knowledge to engage with new material.
- Learners learn more than we explicitly present to them.
- Learners can teach, correct and learn from each other.
- Learners need time, practice and regular recycling to assimilate lesson input.
- Learners need motivation, challenge and work in order to learn.
- Learners have diverse needs and wants.
- Learners learn and respond in different ways.

Chapter **1**

Starting Off

It is of vital importance to get things right from the very beginning, so that you can establish the atmosphere for the whole course, making judicious use of control and laying down efficient procedures that, in the long run, will save a great deal of time.

Getting the balance right

The critical word for starting off with a new class is 'balance'. Exactly how to get the balance right is impossible to prescribe, but being aware of the variables, and understanding what makes them vary, are important first steps. In many teaching environments, discipline is the main preoccupation, and here the balance might be a combination of being firm with being friendly.

In other areas, balance is necessary between a sense of purpose and a sense of enjoyment, teacher-talk and student-talk, showing you care about your learners and encouraging them and challenging them to take responsibility for their progress.

By the end of the first lesson, you want the following:

- rules and routines to be established
- administrative records to be up and running
- to have introduced yourself and to have given the students the chance to introduce themselves
- to have allowed learners to express a little of what they know
- to have allowed them to express what their expectations are
- to have presented some new input or at least practised some areas of the target language.

The students' needs and wants have to be juggled and aligned with your own perceptions and priorities, as well as your own needs and wants. You must show signs of organisational ability, subject knowledge, sensitivity to learners and a cool, flexible ability to cope with the unexpected. The atmosphere should be friendly and productive, to make the students 'come back for more', but also serious, to the extent that when they come back they have the necessary materials, they have completed the homework and they follow the rules and routines agreed on the first day.

And all this in the first lesson. No wonder you took up teaching for a challenge!

Here are some suggestions for achieving the right balance, in line with MINIMAX principles:

- Reduce teacher input in favour of student output.
- Share the limelight where possible, but without applying undue pressure.
- Concentrate on input that goes a long way.
- Improve your organisation, which leads to longer term efficiency.
- Show that your students' needs are being catered for.
- Allow them different channels of feedback to you.

These objectives are mutually achievable. If students are encouraged to participate, the lesson will feel productive and purposeful, and disruptive behaviour is less likely. If the focus is on the students, they have more chance to produce language, and will perceive the lesson as relevant to them. If learners' needs are sought, and opinions heeded, they will see that the teacher cares about their involvement and progress. When students are engaged, they enjoy themselves without necessarily being conscious of it. If they see underlying control and order, they will feel more secure and have more direction.

Learning names

This is an important means of control, and it is worth aiming to know all your students' names after the first session. Knowing a name is the best way to draw an individual's attention to something. This is useful for defusing undesirable situations early and it helps you to keep records and to plan activities (so you can avoid the use of 'You, you and you, work together'). It makes the students feel part of the group, and that the teacher recognises their personal involvement (they are not just another body in another chair). Finally, it helps you to deal efficiently with department heads and parents, when situations such as phone calls, progress enquiries, discipline procedures, and so on, occur. And many of these do crop up in the early stages.

Strategies for learning names include:

- class activities or games (see Activities 1 and 2)
- name badges or putting name cards on tables
- drawing a classroom plan and recording the names in the positions where you were first introduced to the students (it doesn't matter if they change later)
- encouraging students to use each other's names
- selecting activities which encourage discovery about each other and involve reporting back to the class (Activity 3).

It is worthwhile going over your list before the second lesson, to see how many faces you can put to the names, and any other information you can recall.

Breaking the ice

Switching the focus onto the students must be done with sensitivity. Students might appreciate a choice or an opt-out option, and they may prefer breaking the ice with their neighbours before addressing the whole class.

Instead of asking your students to introduce themselves to the whole class, get them to interview a partner and later introduce them to the class.

Ice-breakers encourage students to lose inhibitions by playing games or by speaking, in the protected environment of activity and noise, to a small number of listeners (Activities 4-6, amongst others).

Building team spirit

The quicker a group get to know each other, the more relaxed the atmosphere will be and the more they can refer to each other during activities: more personalised information can be used, making sessions meaningful and memorable (Activities 7-12). Team-building suggests grouping class members into smaller units for an activity, involving working together and often competing with other units.

Problem-solving, puzzles, quizzes and competitions all help to bond people towards a common goal, while they learn about each other and have fun at the same time. Most activities will include some linguistic content, and so the group will be learning while they establish social contact and rapport. Rapport with the teacher will grow indirectly, as students are enjoying the content and the company of the class. Do not expect these things to happen all on the first day, but results are more likely to be better in a class who 'hit it off' early.

An excellent team-building game which focuses on the students' personal information is Activity 13, and it would also serve well as an ice-breaker. Alternatively, a team quiz is an effective way to start, and a quiz on British (or other appropriate) culture or on the English language would work well at the start of a new course. In true MINIMAX style, of course, the teams would pool their own questions (see Chapter 3).

Discovering what they know

Finding out what students remember or already know seems a natural way to foster learning, and this can be done from the first day, even with a beginners' class (Activity 14). It allows the student to contribute, it gives the teacher useful information, and it transfers the focus onto the students. Again, students who are shy or wary of exposure may prefer to contribute in pairs or small groups rather than to the whole class, and groupwork might take care of excitable students who may otherwise dominate the activity.

Analysing their needs

Needs Analysis is the process of finding out what your students need, or at least what they think they need, at the start of a course (and not just at the start). It includes a diagnosis of current strengths and weaknesses, an investigation into reasons for attending classes, language objectives and learning preferences.

Why are these important? Because they help you decide how and what to teach. If pronunciation is a weakness, you can devote time to it; if students need to brush up their English for an impending visit, you can focus on language for the trip; if an objective is to gain confidence on the telephone, you can practise that; if students are unfamiliar with particular educational practices, such as pairwork, you can ease them in with explanations and demonstrations. If you don't have any of this information, you are left teaching in a vacuum, only guessing at what is useful.

Furthermore, conducting Needs Analysis shows the students that their priorities are being listened to, as long as you respond to the findings in your syllabus planning. As far as the method is concerned, here are some alternatives:

Interviews

This may be difficult in class time, but in many schools an oral interview is part of the placement procedure before classes are formed. It is a good opportunity to find out students' preferences, and may even help to place students in appropriate classes. In other words, students can be grouped according to their objectives and interests (such as exam preparation) as well as their language level.

If you can interview your own class, use a checklist to work through, keeping notes as you go (you could use a questionnaire). You may save yourself a great deal of time and stress by knowing some information about your students, as you can probe into attitude and behaviour, as well as strengths and weaknesses.

Discussion
On the first day the class could have an open Needs Analysis discussion, with the main points summarised on posters, the board or OHP transparencies.

Discussion could be organised in groups, after which each group makes a presentation to the class. To involve more individuals, the discussion can start off in pairs which later merge to form larger groups. This is known as a *Pyramid Debate* (Activity 15).

Questionnaires
A useful activity for your first lesson with a class might be to ask them to fill in a Needs Analysis questionnaire.

Questionnaires needn't be a silent, individual activity, as students can interview each other, note down their partner's responses and finally report back to you and the rest of the group (Activity 16).

An example of a questionnaire which you could adapt for your own purposes is *Welcome to your English Class!* (see page 25).

Investigating diverse learning styles

Learners learn in different ways and respond differently to educational stimuli according to multiple intelligences or sensitivities. An efficient teacher will therefore try and offer a variety of channels of learning, and in order to do that will need to find out as much as possible about their students, as early as possible. As well as ascertaining information about jobs, subject preferences and hobbies, a quiz such as the one on page 79 (*Learner Sensitivities Questionnaire*) can be useful for raising awareness for teacher and student alike. (See Chapter 6 for a more detailed discussion of this issue.)

Asserting control

The issue that causes most stress in teaching is that of classroom control. It may start as simply fear of the unknown, in that teachers frequently worry about the behaviour of a class before meeting them (particularly young learners, and this includes children and teenagers). From the very start, teachers need to be clear about ground rules, their approach to the class, discipline and drawing the line between acceptable and unacceptable conduct. It is usually this clarity which gives teachers confidence to take and keep control, so that effective learning can proceed.

Efficient classroom control can mean a smooth, enjoyable and productive course, if the right steps are taken almost inconspicuously at the right time.

These steps might include the following:

- Let the students know what is unacceptable before it happens.
- Act quickly and firmly in response to unacceptable behaviour.
- Avoid confrontation, taking things personally or getting personal.
- Balance openness with confidentiality.
- Always act in the students' interests.
- Keep good records and show them when necessary.
- Establish routines, such as getting silence, setting and collecting homework, etc.
- Have everyone's attention before explaining instructions.
- Make sure everyone knows what to do.
- Offer a varied programme and keep everyone busy.
- Maintain an atmosphere of progress and improvement.
- Give praise where it is due.

Being organised

Few teachers would disagree that being organised holds the key to success in many areas of teaching. It is an effective way of earning students' confidence and respect, and of preventing potential problems of behaviour. It also makes your life much easier! If you establish certain routines early, such as groupwork and procedures for changing groups, or ways of achieving silence, then you will save yourself time, effort and stress later. Here is a list of suggestions. To what extent would they fit in with your style of teaching?

Marking

- Encourage students to check their work and even 'edit' it before you take it in.
- Do the marking as soon as it comes in, and get it back promptly.
- Keep a file for marking, and make sure students' names are on their work.

Assessment

- Keep a record of all student output.
- Assess work for more than just accuracy; aspects such as content, task, style, thought, thoroughness, presentation and punctuality are also important.
- Keep attendance records, including lateness.

Paperwork

- File all your material.
- Always put papers back in the right file.
- Cut down on photocopying (see Chapter 4).

Classroom management

- Make sure the classroom is as you want it before the students come in.
- Have all your materials ready before going into class.
- Test your equipment before the lesson.
- Write clearly and show good examples of the quality of work you expect.
- Establish routines for changing activities, moving furniture, achieving silence, etc.
- Tell students when homework is due - and stick to your schedule.

Maintaining productivity

- Decide which jobs can be delegated, drawing up a rota.
- Have a self-access box (see Chapter 6) and other materials (eg. magazines) available in class
- Foster study skills, such as using a dictionary, storing notes, etc.

Conclusion

If you allow unacceptable practice to creep in unchecked, this is likely to have repercussions and create a great deal of work and stress later on. If students know what to expect and where to draw the line, and understand that you are in control of the situation from the start, they are more likely and willing to co-operate and participate productively and happily. They will accept the balance without rocking the boat.

Activity 1

Names Circle

Level	Any
Aims	Learning names
Duration	5-10 minutes
Materials	A ball of paper, if you play *The Ball Game*
Preparation	None

Procedure

1. Stand in a circle with your students, and ask each person to say their name. With large classes, you can make two or more circles.

2. The first student says their own name, the second says the first student's name and their own, the third student says the first and second students' names and then their own, and so on. If someone can't remember a name, elicit help from the group.

Variations

1. *Torpedo*: Demonstrate by walking into the centre of the circle, change direction and walk much more quickly towards a student, saying their name. This student then does the same to another student, and so on.

2. *The Ball Game*: Everyone stands in a circle.
   Round 1: Throw a ball of paper to one of your students, and encourage that student to do the same. Each student says their name when they catch the ball.
   Round 2: Each student says the name of the student they throw the ball to.

Notes

In this activity, there are two stages: saying one's own name, and saying other students' names. The first stage presents the names, the second stage tests the memory and also helps to remind students of names they haven't yet learnt.

Activity 2

Names Crossword

Level	Any
Aims	Practising names; revising personal information
Duration	20 minutes
Materials	Optional: Wordsearch grids (page 46) / OHP transparencies
Preparation	None

Procedure

1. Divide the class into groups of three to six students.

2. Ask each group to list the names of all the students in the class. With a large class, you can limit the number of names.

3. The students fit the names into an interlocking pattern. Blank Wordsearch grids (see page 46) are helpful for this.

4. They make a copy of the pattern, without the names, and insert crossword numbers.

5. They then write clues, based on information they already know about their new classmates. (Alternatively, the clues could be read aloud to the whole class.)

6. The blank crossword is presented on the board, on a poster or on an OHP, together with the clues.

7. The other groups have to solve the crossword puzzle.

Variation

Hangman and *Anagrams* are both game formats which, like *Wordsearch*, can be used successfully with students' names.

Notes

Grids help speed up the creation of the crossword plan. Remember that the important language work takes place in the design of clues.

Activity 3

Interactive Survey

Level	Intermediate onwards
Aims	Ice-breaker; asking questions about personal information
Duration	30 minutes
Materials	Slips of paper, each bearing a student's name
Preparation	1 minute

Procedure

1. Each student writes a question they would like to ask everybody in the class (ie. the same question to all the students).
2. They mingle, asking their questions, recording the answers and noting the name of each interviewee.
3. Each student picks a slip of paper with another student's name on it.
4. They mingle again and ask for all the responses given by the student they have been 'allocated'.
5. They write up the information about their student in the form they choose, eg. notes, essay, dialogue, poem, etc.
6. The final versions are read out or displayed.

Variation

For display, students can write on coloured paper and include diagrams, photos, etc.

Notes

1. If students are stuck for ideas, suggest some yourself, eg:
    - *Why did you decide to join this class?*
    - *Why are you learning English?*
    - *How do you feel about being here now?*

   Other useful topics are hobbies, English, travel, likes and dislikes, family, career, experiences, etc.
2. This activity is excellent for staff induction, too.

Activity 4

Tea or Coffee?

Level	Intermediate onwards
Aims	Ice-breaker; practising giving reasons and opinions
Duration	10 minutes
Materials	None
Preparation	None

Procedure

1. The class stands facing you in a suitable space.
2. Explain that there is an imaginary line down the middle of the space. With a big group, the line might be a strip you can call a 'speech-free zone'.
3. On the line, or in the strip, nobody is allowed to speak.
4. At a given signal, the students move to one side of the line or the other. The signal is a simple choice of two words, given by you. One choice (eg. *tea*) is one side of the line, the other choice (eg. *coffee*) is the other.
5. The students stand on their chosen side and ask the nearest person why they made that choice.
6. When they have finished speaking, they come back to the line.
7. Be very strict about the 'no speaking' rule.
8. When everyone is back on the line and silent, give the next choice.

Variation

The students might like to suggest their own choices.

Notes

1. You create the choices according to the topics you wish to work on. This activity is useful for introducing or concluding a theme, eg. *beach or mountain, bath or shower, film or book, night or day, work or study, radio or TV, piano or computer, sport or art*, etc.
2. Avoid students' talking in groups. Pairs are preferable.
3. Encourage changing partners.
4. If only one student moves to one of the sides, you can step in and talk to them.

Activity 5

Three Five Seven

Level	Beginner onwards
Aims	Energiser; revising numbers
Duration	15 minutes
Materials	None
Preparation	None

Procedure

1. Ask everyone to stand in a circle.
2. Practise numbers in sequence first. Start by saying a number yourself and consecutive students say the next number.
3. Introduce an action (eg. waving both hands) to be performed every time *'five'* or a multiple of 5 is said. Practise this round the circle.
4. Introduce a second action (eg. turning 360 degrees on the spot) for every time *'seven'*, a multiple of 7, or any number containing 7 is said. Practise. (Don't forget that both actions will have to be done for 35.)
5. Introduce the rule that every time *'seven'* (etc.) is said (ie. when someone turns 360°), you change direction around the circle (the numbers still increase). Practise.
6. The game element is that from now on, there is a penalty. Students making mistakes will drop out by sitting down.
7. When the game is down to the last two players, there can be no reversing of direction. For a quick finish, introduce a new action (eg. pulling a face) for *'three'* and all multiples and numbers containing 3.

Variations

1. If dropping out seems too harsh, 'lives' can be lost instead. Each student has three lives, and can therefore make three mistakes before having to drop out.
2. You can vary the actions, as you wish.

Notes

This is a variation on a well-known party game called *Fizz-buzz*, in which the words *fizz* and *buzz* substitute 5 and 7. It's great fun but, linguistically, it is better to keep the numbers in the game and introduce actions.

Activity 6

Banana, Banana, Banana

Level	Beginner onwards
Aims	Energiser; practising pronunciation; revising food vocabulary
Duration	10-15 minutes
Materials	None
Preparation	None

Procedure

1. Everyone sits in a circle, but you stand in the centre without a chair.
2. Each student names a fruit or vegetable. Do your best to remember them.
3. The aim of the game is to get out of the centre and onto a seat.
4. To do this, you have to choose one of the fruits or vegetables and say it three times before the relevant student can say it once. For example, if you want to oust the student who chose *pear* from their seat, you say *'pear, pear, pear'* before they can say *'pear'*.
5. If you succeed, the student comes into the centre and takes on your role. You sit down and take up the position of 'pear'.
6. If you don't succeed, you stay in the middle and keep trying.
7. The winner is the last student to be moved.

Variation

You can vary the vocabulary topic.

Notes

It is important to keep it snappy. Don't allow long silences.

Activity 7
Pass the Poster

Level	Elementary onwards
Aims	Reinforcing knowledge about each other
Duration	10 minutes
Materials	One sheet of A3 or A4 paper per student
Preparation	None

Procedure

1. Arrange the class in a circle, or several circles, and give each student a sheet of paper.
2. Ask the students to write their name and draw something which represents them, eg. a self-portrait, an outline of their hand, their favourite possession, etc.
3. They all pass their posters to the left, and write something on each poster about the student whose poster it is.
4. The posters are passed to everybody in the circle until they get back to the original student.
5. Display the posters, if you wish.

Variation

You can provide coloured pens, so that each student writes in a different colour. The finished posters are then bright and colourful and look good on the wall.

Notes

1. If it takes a lot of effort to arrange the classroom for circles, you might like to keep it that way for the whole session, and do other activities which also require circles, such as Activities 12 and 20.
2. The students need to know a little about each other, so this activity works well at the end of the first lesson or at the start of the second.

Activity 8
Silhouettes

Level	Beginner onwards
Aims	Getting to know each other
Duration	15 minutes
Materials	Lining paper stuck onto the wall; coloured pens
Preparation	None

Procedure

1. Ask the students in turn to stand against the wall, while someone else traces round their silhouette onto the lining paper, with a pencil.
2. Each student selects a coloured pen and goes over their outline. They should write onto their silhouette three things they like, eg. family, music, sports, etc.
3. They mingle and write on each other's silhouette any information they know about them.

Variation

If wall space is limited, it may be better to do Activity 7 *Pass the Poster.*

Notes

1. If everyone writes in a different colour, the effect is very bright, and if they write only within the silhouettes, their outline stands out more.
2. It is better to start with pencil, to avoid getting ink on people's clothes and hair.

Activity 9

A Physical Map

Level	Any
Aims	Ice-breaker; practising speaking
Duration	10 minutes
Materials	Lots of room!
Preparation	None

Procedure

1. Find or clear a large area.
2. Explain that the floor is a world map.
3. Stand on an appropriate spot and say that you are standing on the place where you are from.
4. Encourage the students to stand on spots representing their home towns.
5. They will need to talk to each other in order to do this.
6. Encourage each student to say a little to the whole class about their home area whilst still standing on the relevant spot.

Variations

1. If the class are from the same country, it can be a map of that country.
2. Alternatively, it can be a city map.
3. If you don't have such a large floorspace, use the board, where each student should mark their hometown.

Notes

1. Curiosity about geography and the fun of forming a physical map should remove a lot of the fear of talking to a group.
2. This simple idea is deeply personalised, and students usually learn and remember a good deal about each other.

Activity 10

Autobiographical Jigsaws

Level	Intermediate onwards
Aims	Getting to know each other
Duration	30 minutes
Materials	A copy of your autobiography for each group
Preparation	20 minutes (the first time you do the activity, to prepare the autobiography)

Procedure

1. Divide the class into groups of three to four students.
2. Give each group a copy of your autobiography, cut into pieces.
3. The groups have to put it in order, working together.
4. Ask them to justify the order.
5. Encourage them to write their own autobiographies in separable parts.
6. They cut up the autobiographies. The rest of the group to put them in order.
7. The groups consult with the authors to check if the order is correct.
8. Encourage the groups to justify the order to you.
9. The final versions can be glued onto cards and displayed on the wall.

Variation

The autobiography can be written in the first or third person.

Notes

1. Once the materials are prepared, remember to keep them for future use.
2. Remember that the order can vary but still be coherent and acceptable, even if it doesn't match the original autobiography.
3. Chronology, topic and linking expressions (eg. *it, this, so, therefore,* etc.) help to order the texts.

Activity 11
Quantifier Survey

Level	Intermediate onwards
Aims	Practising speaking; questions and quantifiers
Duration	20 minutes
Materials	Enough copies of the *Quantifier Survey Statements* to allow one statement per student (or group of students)
Preparation	1 minute (for the photocopies)

Procedure

1. Give out one of the *Quantifier Survey Statements* to each student or group of students.
2. The students read their statements. Make sure they understand them.
3. Their task is to find out if the statement is true, so they need to prepare a question (or questions) to ask other students, eg. *Do you live near here?* or *Where do you live?*
4. They mingle and collect responses.
5. They count up their responses and decide if the statement is true.
6. If it is not true, they must create a sentence which is true for the class.
7. Each student or group reports their findings, explaining with statistics, eg.
   '19 out of 20 students live within one kilometre of the school, so it is true to say that most of us live near here.'
8. Encourage the class to write a record of their findings, eg. on the board, OHP, handout, poster, etc.

Variation

Alternative statements on any subject can be dictated to the class (eg. crime: *None of us believes in the death penalty.*)

Notes

This particular set of statements is useful for an early lesson with a new class. It helps students to get to know each other and gives you useful background information.

DESIGNED TO PHOTOCOPY

Quantifier Survey Statements

Most of us live near here.

Some of us have been abroad.

None of us has lived abroad.

We all like studying English.

Not many of us
speak English every day.

Almost all of us
need English in our jobs.

A few of us prefer
English to other subjects.

Everybody here
watches TV in English.

Very few of us
read novels in English.

Nobody here has
English-speaking friends.

Activity 12

Chair Invitations

Level	Elementary onwards
Aims	Practising relative clauses
Duration	10 minutes
Materials	None
Preparation	None

Procedure

1. The students arrange their chairs in a circle which includes you, with one empty chair on your right.
2. Demonstrate first yourself. Indicating the empty chair, say *'I'd like someone who is (wearing black jeans) to come and sit here'*.
3. The student with black jeans (there should only be one) gets up and sits in the chair.
4. This leaves a different chair empty, so the student on the left of the chair has to invite someone over by means of a similar sentence.
5. The game continues at least until everyone has moved to a different chair.

Variation

The invitation could be *'I'd like you to sit here because ... '*.

Notes

1. Encourage students to vary the sentence structure. This activity is not intended to be a drill of *is wearing*.
2. Insist on accurate, full sentences. Don't allow isolated utterances, such as *'black jeans'*.

Activity 13

Shaved Eyebrows

Level	Intermediate onwards
Aims	Teambuilding; enquiring about personal information
Duration	20 minutes
Materials	None
Preparation	None

Procedure

1. Divide the class into groups of three students.
2. Each group discusses secrets or strange experiences in private.
3. They choose one incident or secret for the group.
4. When everybody is ready, the first group faces the class, and reveals the strange incident, but not who it happened to.
5. Each member of the group tells a story about the circumstances of this incident as if it happened to them personally. Two will invent the story, the other tells the true story.
6. The class have to find out who this incident really happened to, by asking appropriate questions.
7. The audience make a guess, and the speakers reveal the truth.

Variation

The audience can ask questions to each speaker to probe further.

Notes

The name of this activity comes from the very first time I encountered it. One of my group had once shaved his eyebrows!

Activity 14

Beginners' Brainstorm

Level	Beginners (first lesson)
Aims	Inspiring confidence; eliciting existing lexical knowledge
Duration	30 minutes
Materials	None
Preparation	None

Procedure

1. The students write down individually any words they already know in English (five minutes, maximum). Help everyone to write something, even if it is just a name, such as *London.*
2. Form pairs. The students exchange their items and write them down.
3. Join the pairs to form groups of four, and continue the exchange.
4. Break the groups up and form new groups of four.
5. Collate the list on the blackboard/whiteboard/OHP/ poster. Make sure everyone makes a copy.

Variation

When you regroup, it can become a competition to see who can complete the list first.

Notes

1. A 'beginners' class is often a mixture of levels, and this diversity is exploited in this activity. It is important that everyone writes, because they will be separated when they form new groups. Also, each student will then have something to share.
2. In a monolingual class, the mother tongue can be used to translate if necessary.
3. A MINIMAX teacher would involve the students in collating the final list.
4. As the input comes from the students, you can circulate, help, offer suggestions and make sure everyone knows what to do.
5. This activity generates lots of vocabulary. Keep it, as it will prove very useful, eg. for later revision, displaying it on the wall, using it for categorisation activities and playing numerous wordgames.

Activity 15

Needs Analysis Pyramid

Level	Elementary onwards
Aims	Ice-breaking; identifying needs, priorities and preferences of a new class; encouraging oral fluency
Duration	20 minutes
Materials	None
Preparation	None

Procedure

1. Write a list of language areas on the board. My list is:
    - Grammar
    - Vocabulary
    - Pronunciation
    - Speaking practice
    - Listening to cassettes
    - Listening to people
    - Reading
    - Writing
2. Divide the class into pairs.
3. Ask each pair to discuss their priorities amongst the list you have written.
4. They must agree on an order of priority.
5. Combine the pairs to make groups of four. They, too, have to discuss and agree on an order of priority.
6. Combine the groups again and repeat the process until finally it becomes a whole-class discussion.

Variations

1. The list could be based on classroom procedures, eg. games, video, grammar, exercises, storytelling, songs, pairwork, exam practice, drama, dictation.
2. Instead of putting the eight priorities in order, students can pick out the three most important, as long as they agree on them.
3. Pyramid debates like this can be done on almost any topic.

Notes

The repetition of discussion helps to build speaking confidence. Starting in pairs involves more individuals and allows quieter students to participate in a sheltered way.

Activity 16

Needs Analysis Questionnaire

Level	Elementary onwards
Aims	Identifying the needs, priorities and preferences of a new class; encouraging oral fluency; enabling students to get to know each other
Duration	20-30 minutes
Materials	One questionnaire per student
Preparation	5 minutes

Procedure

1. Give a copy of the *Welcome to your English Class!* questionnaire on page 25 to each student.
2. Divide the class into pairs: Student A and Student B. If there is an odd number, make one group of three (with Student C).
3. Explain that the answers they write are their partner's answers, *not* their own.
4. Student A interviews Student B, and vice versa. They record the responses on the questionnaire, preferably in complete sentences. (In the group of three, A interviews B, B interviews C, and C interviews A.)
5. Each student then introduces their partner to the class, mentioning some of the information contained in the questionnaire.
6. The class have an opportunity to ask questions about the student who has just been introduced to them.
7. Collect the questionnaires, making sure the name of the writer is supplied.

Variations

1. You may prefer each student to fill in their own questionnaire as a quiet activity at the end of the lesson, especially with a boisterous class.
2. If there isn't time to do this in class, the class could fill in the questionnaire for homework. An appropriate homework might be to ask the class to write about themselves. They won't be short of content!

Notes

This activity is excellent for practising reported speech. It also gives you an early indication of writing competence.

DESIGNED TO PHOTOCOPY

Welcome to your English Class!

Name: .... Class: .... Time: ....

Where do you live?

What are your interests/hobbies?

How long have you been learning English?

Where have you been learning English?

Do you enjoy English?

In what situations do you need to speak English?

Do you read or write in English in your free time?

Do you watch films/TV in English?

Why are you learning English?

What do you like about English classes?

Is there anything you don't like about English classes?

Have you ever been to an English-speaking country?

What job do you do/would you like to do?

Why is it important to speak English in class?

How can you improve your English outside the classroom without the teacher?

What exams (if any) would you like to take in English?

How do you want your English to improve?

Are there any other comments you would like to make?

Chapter **2**

Personalisation

Encouraging student involvement helps to make learning more personally relevant, tasks more meaningful and often inspires motivation, as well as saving preparation time. The message transmitted to students is that they are important and interesting, and that they will see language developing around their personal contribution.

Personalisation

This means encouraging students to bring information about themselves into lesson activity. Teachers also personalise whenever they share information about themselves. In both cases, the information is usually more meaningful because it relates directly to the immediate environment, compared to information about external or abstract things. Personal exchanges also have affective value, breaking down barriers and inhibitions. Furthermore, the authenticity of personal information is such that it cannot be questioned: the teacher has no power over its truthfulness, so that there is a real information gap. Learners may logically enjoy describing people or places they know rather than go through the motions of describing materials in coursebooks or in photographs which the teacher may have taken a lot of trouble to provide.

You may present new language in a number of ways, but using information about yourself or your students is a very natural and memorable way to practise it quite early in the course. To illustrate *going to*, you might start by talking about some of your own plans. To illustrate the simple present tense, you can make statements about where students live, or what they like. In this way, the students are learning about each other and about you as they learn English.

If you want to practise dates, students' birthdays provide appropriate content; ask them to stand in a line and get in order from January to December, but they must organise it themselves, using only English, of course (Activity 17). You will decide how much modelling, drilling and general assistance to provide, and when. But the target structure may be remembered simply because they got up and did it and it was about them.

Teachers may worry that personalisation involves a risk, in that you don't know what will come up, and therefore can't control it. However, the important thing is to take an interest in their replies, rather than only concentrating on the structure you want to model. You want to practise *he/she's got ...,* so you ask your students if they have a television, and one of them says *'no'*. Avoid dismissing this reply as unsuitable for your purposes: instead, show interest, surprise even. This is real communication, and authentic reactions are valuable. You will get round to your structure *Mohammed's got a television* eventually, and even if nobody in the class has one, you can introduce people you know in your presentation. Later on you can make use of personalised examples from the class by including the negative replies in your presentation of the negative structure.

It is probable that in a real target-language situation, students will talk about themselves, ask questions relevant to themselves or give their own opinions. It seems logical, therefore, to encourage them to invest themselves in lessons now, as that is what they will be doing naturally later.

Imagination

Why is it important to tap into our students' imaginations? Firstly, although there is usually a syllabus to follow, students will want new language for anything they feel is necessary or desired. The 'real' syllabus will respond to what is in the students' heads as well as what is written in the programme.

Secondly, encouraging students to use their imagination makes learning fun and adds interest to the lesson for everybody. It is arguably more stimulating to learn new words by using them creatively in a game or story than by consciously memorising a list. Furthermore, a simple lexical list is unlikely to carry connotational or collocational information, compared to using the words to create larger linguistic units.

Finally, we can use what is in our learners' heads for lesson content. This can include building our presentation on top of what they already know, shaping letter-writing according to what they want to say, brainstorming ideas for later analysis and processing, and designing activities for each other.

Memory

Memory, like muscle, develops with use: recall and retention are self-reinforcing. Lessons should involve frequent recycling in varied and stimulating conditions relevant to the learners. Memory is also closely linked to the imagination: stimulating experiences are memorable. All this means that students will remember language better if it is perceived as useful or important, if they are required to recall it frequently and if input and practice involve the self, the imagination or the emotions.

Combined strategies

Here are a number of strategies which combine the above elements of personalisation, imagination and memory.

Eliciting

Sometimes, when you present new language, all eyes are on you, and the students may be quite passive. If you elicit as much as possible, it will activate your audience.

To present a situational dialogue in a restaurant, ask for contributions from the students to set it up; they can guess what the situation is, suggest how many diners there are, give the exact location, say what time of day it is, offer names for the customers, waiter/waitress and restaurant, show the seating arrangement, describe the people and the dining room, describe what type of restaurant it is, how the table is decorated, the choices available on the menu, the qualities of the chef, and so on. This is not wasting time, it is involving students in the presentation, activating language practice and memory recall, and allowing you to build new language onto what is revealed as existing knowledge. And as well as being motivating and possibly challenging, it takes the focus away from you, the teacher. Sometimes, therefore, the less you say the better.

Eliciting also boosts students' confidence, because what was perplexing and new last lesson is shown to be remembered, and can be drawn out of the students' memories to show a clearer picture. Learners may balk at the present simple interrogative, but ask them to repeat the pattern the next day and they will rise to the challenge. And if you include a few deliberate mistakes, it is rewarding to see them correct you.

Brainstorming

This is an established technique with diverse possibilities, but the basic idea is to encourage recall of items connected to a common criterion or theme. It recycles language in a safe context, as students pool contributions without, at first, criticising or rejecting any. Once pooled, items can be sorted. The advantage is that students learn from each other, even from inappropriate contributions, as they discuss why they are not acceptable. The activity can be timed, or you can specify how many items should be aimed for if you want to introduce a competitive element. In general it is a quick way to find out what students already know so that new material can be developed from their input. Again, you are involving the students in your presentations.

Here are some examples:

- *What words do you already know in English?* (Activity 14)
- *Brainstorm an item for every letter of the alphabet.* (Activity 18)
- *Brainstorm clothes vocabulary* (eg. before presenting shopping dialogues).
- *Find as many uses as possible for a used cork/empty flowerpot/cabbage.*
- *How many Shakespearean characters can you name?*
- *Write a list of things which are round/blue/can fly/have four legs.*
- *Find things which everybody in the group likes/nobody likes.*
- *What tasks does a carpenter do?*
- *What have we studied this week?*
- *What different things does your company do (if you work in a company)?*

From these few examples it should be clear how much language, discussion, analysis, personal investment, resourcefulness and memory recall can be produced from a simple instruction.

Once lists are produced, they can be exploited. Don't waste all this information! Items can be singled out for explanation, they can be compared, prioritised, put in order, put to the vote, and so on, as well as being used in your next presentation.

Passing it on

This is an important element of student-generated activities (see Chapter 3), as work is passed round to recycle language. In many other activities, too, groups receive input from preceding groups and then respond or modify it in some way:

- A list of vocabulary brainstormed by the preceding group can be represented as a picture by the new group. (Activity 37)
- A tale can be passed on orally, and the listener embellishes it in some way before passing it on. (Activity 19)
- A story can be built up by passing it round and each group continues it. (Activity 20)

The advantages of this procedure should be made clear. If work is passed on, everybody sees it. If students know their work is going to be shown to other students (and it is a good idea to tell them at the outset) they will take greater pains, if only in presentation, to ensure that it is legible. The following group react to the stimulus provided by their peers, not the teacher, and they respond in their own way.

Often in class students produce output which is not made relevant to other students. Much language is produced for its own sake, and doesn't involve the listener or the reader. In writing a 'pass it on' story there is a reason to read, in order to know how to continue, and there is a reason to write, because you know someone else will be reading it later. After completion there is a further reason to read to see how the story, which contains students' personal contributions, ends up. Similarly, in oral storytelling, there are reasons to listen and to speak (Activities 19, 81 and 87).

Guessing

Encouraging guessing is fun and challenging and it recycles a lot of language. Rather than doing all the talking, the teacher can hide, tease and elicit. If you use a photograph in class, for example, you can create extra interest and curiosity by asking the group to guess what it is, and develop the intrigue by revealing it slowly or only in part.

Here is a brief list of possible applications:

- The teacher conceals an object or picture.
- The teacher is thinking of a word.
- Students conceal information from each other.
- Students guess each other's responses to an exercise or questionnaire.
- The teacher writes/draws on the board slowly: students guess what it is.
- mime games (Activity 22)
- puzzle stories, mysteries
- finding information using *Yes/No* questions only
- guessing games, eg. *Twenty Questions*
- Guess if your partner is lying or not. (Activity 30)

Guessing (when there's nothing there)

This sounds unfair, but it can generate much enjoyable language practice from little preparation. One technique involves telling a story which builds on elicited contributions, chosen by the storyteller from among those offered. Another variation is to build up a story by asking *Yes/No* questions which are answered according to a code (Activity 23).

If you need a photograph but can't find just the right one, take a blank sheet of paper into class. Invite the class to guess the concealed contents, recycling as much language as appropriate. Give clues and guidance as the 'image' approximates towards the objective, dictated by the target language required. When the elicitation is finished, place the 'picture' in an envelope for later. When the time comes, ask the group to recap on the contents: the more demanding you are, the more insistent and detailed will be their contributions, and the greater their surprise when they find there is nothing inside but a blank piece of paper.

The advantages are that they have practised and revised the language you intended and have engaged in real communication. You have had the chance, if you wished, to challenge the confident members by rejecting their suggestions and give confidence to the 'weaker' students by accepting theirs, and this can be reinforced at the recap stage, by allowing these students to reiterate information offered by stronger students earlier on. They have enjoyed a motivating activity in which they started with endless choice of language, which narrowed down as they co-operated together to build a picture which is entirely theirs.

Remembering

In the course of a lesson there are plenty of opportunities for testing absorption of information in a light-hearted way (Activity 24):

- If the class have just completed an exercise, try going over it without allowing them to read their answers.
- If you have just wiped the board clean of input material, ask the students what was written there (exact positions and colours can be demanded, appealing to spatial and visual sensitivities).
- If you have just collected some written work, ask one or two students what they wrote about. In each lesson there might be a slot for recapping the previous lesson's input.

Some teachers elicit a weekly summary of work done, while others encourage reflection at the end of each lesson. New knowledge builds on existing knowledge, but you may have had students who don't seem to be learning. One reason may be that they are not given sufficient opportunity to recall and consolidate what has been covered in class, so they always seem to be starting from the beginning.

Predicting

As a pre-reading or pre-listening activity, and to arouse curiosity, it is often interesting to ask prediction questions from the students' imaginations. Give them the title of a song or a text to see if they can predict the content. For the song *Yellow Submarine*, before they know the title or listen to the recording, the students might be asked *'What is the vehicle?', 'Where are they travelling?', 'What begins to play?', 'Who lives next door?'*. The class are not expected to get the correct answer, but now they have the incentive to listen to see if they were correct.

Students have personalised the activity and might enjoy completing their own story before reading or listening to the intended text. They can also be asked to predict things about their partners (Activity 25).

Storytelling/Guided fantasy

This involves telling a simple story in which, at every detail, you ask the listeners to imagine the scenes, 'props' or characters. Later they may be encouraged to write or speak about the story, including their own personal details:

> *'Imagine you are sitting in your favourite chair - describe the chair* - (so each listener imagines a chair in detail) - *in the room you like best - Which room is it? - What's it like? - doing the activity you find most relaxing - What is it? Suddenly you hear a noise - describe the noise - ...'* and so on.

This is a wonderfully relaxing activity and a springboard for generating many possibilities. You might concentrate on emotions (*'What did you feel when you heard the noise?'*) or senses (*'Describe what the potion tasted like.'*), and you can include any number of vocabulary areas (*'Describe the person at the door.'*). As the teacher you will decide what language areas you want your learners to practise, and you will direct the story accordingly.

But you don't need to spend hours planning an elaborate story, the content of which will be of interest mainly to you, because you chose or created it. The students can create their own detail from your skeleton, and make the story come alive for them. If storytelling is important, then you have a different story from each student, which they can tell each other, write down or display on the wall. The possibilities extend and proliferate from a minimal, flexible stimulus; this is what MINIMAX is all about.

'Psychology' games

There are many of these around, but the basic idea is the same. The students record their answers to certain questions, only to find that they have some 'hidden' significance which is revealed later. It makes personal answers even more personal, and the language more memorable. It includes interesting ambiguities, is good to share and often causes hilarity. And it is a good way to encourage often extended written answers and a great deal of reading, as the students show each other their texts. This can be an excellent introduction to creative writing, as it sensitises students towards ambiguity and metaphor (Activity 26).

Open-ended activities

The important things students need to know about vocabulary, such as meaning, collocation, connotation, register, pronunciation and spelling, are generally 'closed', in the sense that the number of correct choices is limited. When it comes to practising the vocabulary with a view to remembering it, open-ended activities are valuable as well as being fun, mainly because they are personalised and cannot be corrected.

As an illustration of a closed activity, put the words *sandwich, lettuce, dessert, ice-cream, rhubarb* and *champagne* into two categories: *1st syllable stress/2nd syllable stress*. This is closed because the choices are either right or wrong, and there is little scope for argument or involvement. An open-ended activity might involve putting them into these groups: *I like it/I don't like it* or *Often/Sometimes/Never*. There is likely to be much more discussion in an open-ended activity, and the teacher can't intervene to say students are wrong about content. This can be extended to include the concept of 'mismatch', which involves associating completely irrelevant sets of vocabulary.

Draw the human body on the board and revise the relevant body parts. Then introduce a list of occupations, and ask how the students would label the body with occupations. Let them label their own mismatches and then compare with each other, giving reasons. Is *lawyer* the brain, the mouth, the pocket? Is *postman* the hand, the feet, the eye?

Label a plan of your bathroom with the above words (*sandwich*, etc.) and justify your labelling. The discussion afterwards might sound surreal (*'I labelled the bathtub 'dessert' as I imagined jumping into custard.'*) but this could imprint the word on the mind forever: the memory responds well to associations of this nature.

Choice

On a more general note, if students can choose their activity or topic, they will be more inclined to want to work with it, even when there is little real choice or when they choose randomly. If the teacher merely assigns work, there may not be an emotional or personal connection for the learner. But if you display four choices, a student may start the thinking process required for the activity at the time of making the choice.

In an activity which involves choosing a photo of a city and considering the advantages and disadvantages of living there (eg. London, New York, Johannesburg or Hong Kong) anyone making a choice would probably start thinking of what they already know and what they could say 'for and against'. Having the choice allows freedom to consider strengths and weaknesses involved in effective task performance.

Also, when a student chooses their photo, even without seeing it, they are more likely to accept and work with it, because they have taken responsibility for it. The teacher must ensure that all photos are appropriate and valuable for the task, so that the student doesn't feel they are left with the bad option.

Conclusion

Although we might give our students something to think about, they will do the thinking themselves, combining their experiences, thoughts and the language they can recall. Consequently, we can save ourselves a great deal of time and effort by allowing the content of our lessons to come from our learners; a truly rich resource if we are willing to discover it. The students' language development will come alive through meaningful, motivating activation, and it has more chance of staying alive this way.

Activity 17
Birthday Line

Level	Elementary onwards
Aims	Ice-breaking; practising saying dates
Duration	5 minutes
Materials	None
Preparation	None

Procedure

1. The students get in a line, in order of their birthdays.

2. You might, if necessary, specify which end of the line is *January*.

Variation

Other criteria for getting in an ordered line could be:
- favourite colours, to be arranged into a rainbow
- time of starting to learn English
- time of getting out of bed
- occupations (general, not the students' own), arranged according to pay, danger, stress, etc.
- how much was eaten for breakfast

Notes

1. You may feel it necessary to highlight problem areas, eg. pronunciation, before starting. Students often find saying times and dates problematic.

2. Guide the students, or leave them with the task to see how they cope, depending on the time available, their level and whether your priority is teambuilding, problem-solving or a quick filler/energiser.

Activity 18
A-Z Brainstorm

Level	Any
Aims	Introducing a topic; revising and sharing vocabulary already known to the group
Duration	15 minutes
Materials	Blank paper
Preparation	None

Procedure

1. Divide the class into pairs or small groups. Each should have a piece of paper.

2. Each group or pair writes out the alphabet in a column down the left margin.

3. Their task is to write a word that starts with each letter of the alphabet. They write it beside the letter.

4. All the words must relate to a common theme, eg. music, animals, etc.

5. The first group to finish is the winner.

Variations

1. If nobody finishes (some letters are virtually impossible), set a time limit. The winners are the ones with the most words.

2. You could extend the vocabulary revision by asking for two or more words for each letter.

Notes

1. Make sure the students know the alphabet. This is a good opportunity to revise it.

2. Don't allow 'proper nouns' at first, as they could fill the list with the names of famous people (eg. pop groups, if the topic is music).

3. The topic you choose will presumably be the one you want to introduce afterwards.

4. If one group finishes this activity well before the others, extend the task to include a second or third word, or proper nouns, eg. the names of relevant people, places, songs, books, etc.

Activity 19

Telling Tales

Level	Intermediate onwards
Aims	Practising storytelling
Duration	30 minutes
Materials	One slip of paper per student
Preparation	None

Procedure

1. Each student invents a character and writes the name on a tiny slip of paper.
2. They invent an everyday incident involving this character, eg. *Fred missed a train and was late for work.*
3. The students stand up, mingle and find a partner. They each tell their tale, and exchange slips.
4. They find another partner. This time they tell the story they have just heard (not their own), adding one or two details. They pass on the corresponding slip.
5. When they have exchanged stories a number of times, they sit in a circle.
6. Invite each student to tell the most recent story, corresponding to the slip of paper in their hand, to the whole class.
7. Ask the originator of each story to tell the original version.

Notes

1. Divide a large class into groups of ten or twelve.
2. Often students find that they have already talked to someone and resist doing so again. They should go ahead, as the stories will be new.
3. By the end of the activity, all the students will have told two stories each to the whole class.
4. In the whole-class session at the end, as each student will have contributed to most or all of the stories, there will be motivation to listen, to hear their own contributions and to see how the story has developed. Also, it is entertaining to see how each story differs from its original.

Activity 20

Crazy Biographies

Level	Elementary onwards
Aims	Getting to know each other; practising narration; revising past tense
Duration	20-40 minutes (variable)
Materials	Blank paper
Preparation	None

Procedure

1. Arrange the students in circles of five or six. Each student writes their first name at the top of a clean sheet of paper, as a title.
2. Ask them to write, in no more than one short paragraph (or two sentences), a brief history of their life up to now, using the third person and the past tense. Even what is true *now* is recorded in the past.
3. Give an example, if necessary: *Susan was born in Prague before her parents moved to Berlin. She went to primary school, learnt German, made many friends, and met her boyfriend David when she was 16.*
4. All the papers are passed to the left. The students continue the biography from their own imaginations. They write two or three sentences.
5. The story is passed on again. Each student adds a short paragraph.
6. Finally, the story reaches the student who started it, who reads it.

Variation

You can vary the number of times the story is passed on, the direction it is passed, and the number of students in each circle.

Notes

1. Each time the story is passed on there is more to read, so allow time for that.
2. The students can correct each other's contributions, or you can correct as you circulate.
3. Allow all the students to read or hear all the stories, eg. by displaying them. There is a good reason to listen or read, as they have all contributed and will be curious to see what happened next.

Activity 21

Design a Monster

Level	Elementary onwards. It works particularly well with young learners.
Aims	Practising animal vocabulary; the present simple tense; possessives (apostrophe *-s*)
Duration	20-30 minutes
Materials	Blank paper, cut into slips
Preparation	10 minutes (to write out the body parts)

Procedure

1. Write out a number of slips of paper, each with the name of a body part of an animal, eg. *trunk, tusks,* etc. (not *eyes, face, feet,* as they are not characteristic).
2. Divide the class into groups of three or four students and give each group between four and eight slips.
3. The groups draw an imaginary monster on a piece of paper (size A4 or A3). It must include all the body parts they have been allocated.
4. The drawings are passed on to another group.
5. Each new group writes a list of the body parts that they think were given out to the first group.
6. The pictures are then passed on again. This time the new group matches the parts of the drawing with the items on the list.
7. Finally, the drawing is passed on or back to the creators of the monster, who check and give feedback on the list and labelling.

Extension

1. The creators now write about their monster: its habits, habitat, diet, etc., on the same piece of paper.
2. The designing team, taking on the role of the monster, can be interviewed by the class.

Variations

1. You can brainstorm the vocabulary of animals and their body parts with the students, who write out the slips of paper themselves.
2. 'Aliens' could be created from assembling human body parts.

Activity 22

Who, What, Where

Level	Elementary onwards
Aims	Practising the vocabulary of occupations and locations; participle clauses; the present continuous tense
Duration	20 minutes
Materials	Blank paper, cut into slips
Preparation	None

Procedure

1. Divide the class into three groups, to prepare the slips: one group writes occupations, one per slip. Another group writes expressions of location, eg. *in the bank, at the swimming pool, underwater, on a bus,* and the last group writes activities, eg. *cleaning your teeth, singing, playing golf, climbing a ladder,* etc.
2. Collect the three sets of slips. Put them in three piles, face down, on a table or chair.
3. Demonstrate the activity first yourself, if necessary.
4. Each student picks one slip from each pile.
5. They now have to mime all three pieces of information at the same time.
6. The rest of the class watch and have to guess the information.

Variation

The mime can be done in pairs or small groups, especially if students are likely to be self-conscious.

Notes

1. Make sure you elicit extended contributions or full sentences, eg. *You are a dentist playing the violin in space.*
2. It is useful to ask the students to write down as many sentences as they can afterwards, to reinforce accuracy.

Activity 23

Crime Story

Level	Intermediate onwards
Aims	Practising *Yes/No* question forms
Duration	15 minutes
Materials	None
Preparation	None

Procedure

1. Ask for a volunteer to leave the room. Before they go, tell them to prepare some *Yes/No* questions to ask about a crime story which you are about to tell the class.

2. Once the volunteer is outside, explain to the rest of the class that there is no story. Instead, there is a code for answering the questions. If the question ends in a consonant, eg. *'Was there a murder?'*, they must say *'Yes'*, and if it ends in a vowel, eg. *'Did somebody die?'*, they say *'No'*.

3. The volunteer comes back into the room and questions the class.

4. Invite the volunteer to tell the story to the class, to their hilarity.

Variations

1. An even better way is to have two volunteers asking their questions to two separate groups. Although they believe the story is the same, it is amusing to hear two very different stories.

2. It doesn't have to be a crime story. Any topic will do.

Notes

1. There is no story, but a story emerges from the volunteer's imagination.

2. This activity is good for recycling vocabulary, so choose a topic you have covered before.

Activity 24

Kim's Game

Level	Elementary onwards
Aims	Practising vocabulary and prepositions of place
Duration	15 minutes
Materials	Blank paper; realia
Preparation	5 minutes (to collect the realia)

Procedure

1. Collect realia of the vocabulary you want to practise. Prepare it on a tray and cover it.

2. Allow the students one minute to look at it.

3. Cover the tray up, and ask the students to list what was there.

Extension

Ask the students to write full sentences describing *where* on the tray the objects are.

Variations

1. The students can work individually or in groups.

2. They can draw a plan of the tray, if they wish, and compare with other students' versions.

Notes

It is in the extension that students are challenged for language production.

Activity 25

Predictable Partner

Level	Elementary onwards
Aims	Practising almost anything; here, it is adjectives and prepositions
Duration	10 minutes
Materials	Blank paper
Preparation	None

Procedure

1 Take a language area from the syllabus or coursebook, eg. collocations of adjectives and prepositions.

2 The students form pairs and, if possible, sit opposite their partner.

3 Ask the following questions:

- *What is your partner most afraid of?*
- *What are they good at?*
- *What are they bad at?*
- *What is the most likely thing they might become addicted to? ... or obsessed with?*
- *What things are they late for?*
- *What do they most worry about?*

4 The students must write full sentences, answering the questions without consulting their partners.

5 Afterwards, they compare their answers with the true details or opinions of their partners.

6 If the coursebook has any exercises on this language point, they could be done afterwards or at home, as reinforcement.

Variation

This can be used for any language area.

Notes

1 There is attention to accuracy because of your prompts, but the students will be engaged in meaning-focused activity.

2 This is a good activity for starting discussions, eg. *addictions*, so it is worth developing it as much as possible.

Activity 26

Hidden Meanings

Level	Intermediate onwards
Aims	Practising vocabulary and writing
Duration	20 minutes
Materials	Blank paper
Preparation	None

Procedure

1 Ask the students to write their answers to the following questions as you say them:

A *What is your favourite animal and why?*
B *What is your second favourite animal and why?*
C *What is your third favourite animal and why?*
D *Write your feelings about the sea.*
E *Write your feelings about coffee.*
F *You are walking and you come to a wall. Describe it. Can you see over it? If so, what can you see?*

2 Give them time to write their answers between the questions.

3 When they have finished, tell them the following analysis. Each answer has a hidden significance:

A *This is how you want other people to see you.*
B *This is how other people see you.*
C *This is what you really are.*
D *This is what you feel about life.*
E *This is how you feel about sex.*
F *The wall represents death.*

4 Encourage the students to share their responses with each other.

Variation

With younger students, you might prefer to use the word *love* rather than *sex* for question E.

Notes

This activity can lead to some unintentionally poetic prose.

Activity 27

You are Your Parent

Level	Intermediate onwards
Aims	Practising speaking unselfconsciously about oneself
Duration	15-20 minutes
Materials	None
Preparation	None

Procedure

1. Divide the class into groups of three or four.
2. In turn, the students talk about themselves to the others in the group, but in the role of someone who knows them well, eg. parent, sibling, partner, friend.
3. Encourage questions from the group to the speaker 'in role'.
4. Every student must speak. Allow five minutes each.

Variations

1. The students might like to guess the relationship after they have listened.
2. A few lies might be included for the group to detect.
3. As well as personal information, the topic could vary, eg. *crime*, and the roleplay still be maintained. After reading a crime story, interview the criminal's mother, brother, spouse, etc.

Notes

It is often easier to reflect and talk about oneself from the point of view of someone else.

Activity 28

Spokesperson

Level	Intermediate onwards
Aims	Practising speaking and question forms
Duration	15 minutes
Materials	None
Preparation	None

Procedure

1. Choose an interesting experience which one of your students has had (consult with the student first).
2. Ask for a volunteer, a different student from the one who had the experience.
3. The volunteer sits in front of the class.
4. Tell the class what the experience was, and who it happened to, and say that this student in front of the class is going to be a 'spokesperson' for the first student.
5. Invite questions from the rest of the class about the experience, eg. details, feelings, etc.
6. The student answers according to what they think the original student would say.
7. Afterwards the original student comments on the answers and offers their own insights and recollections.

Variation

You could have two spokespeople who both answer all the questions, and the original student could say which answers seem to be nearer the truth.

Notes

You may find examples of your students' interesting experiences from conversation, interviews, compositions, and so on.

Activity 29

Photo-Roles

Level	Elementary onwards
Aims	Encouraging oral fluency
Duration	10-30 minutes
Materials	Photos of people (see Note)
Preparation	None (if you have the photos ready)

Procedure

1. Display a photo of a person (famous or otherwise) on the board.
2. Ask for a volunteer to sit beside it and assume the role of the person portrayed.
3. The rest of the class ask questions to the student who is in the role of the person in the photo.
4. The student replies 'in role'.

Variations

1. Portrait paintings can also be used.
2. The picture may be hidden from the class, so that only the volunteer can see it. Later, all the pictures are displayed and the students have to say which student played which role.

Notes

The pictures which work best include thoughtful or emotional subjects, historical time periods, and unusual or surreal situations.

Activity 30

Truth or Lies?

Level	Elementary onwards
Aims	Introducing a new topic; encouraging speaking and guessing
Duration	10-20 minutes
Materials	One slip of paper, marked either *T* or blank, per student
Preparation	5 minutes (to prepare the slips of paper)

Procedure

1. Arrange the class into groups of three or four.
2. Give out the slips of paper and tell the students to keep them hidden.
3. Tell the class you want them to talk about a given topic, eg. their childhood.
4. Those with a *T* tell the truth. Those with blanks include a few lies.
5. When all the members of each group have spoken, ask them to discuss and guess who was lying and who was telling the truth.
6. Those who lied might like to correct the information they gave.
7. If the listeners guessed correctly, they could indicate how they knew.

Variations

1. This particular example can be used to lead into the topics of childhood, family or honesty. Changing the topic of the speaking activity means the activity can introduce almost any topic.
2. To avoid the need for slips of paper, students could be given the choice about whether to lie or not.
3. Alternatively, they could choose to include up to three lies, or none at all.

Notes

1. This activity provides a reason to listen. Students enjoy telling lies. It is imaginative, distorted personalisation.
2. You can deceive classes and give them all blanks (and this saves preparation time) but beware! You can then only use this activity once with each class.

Activity 31
Find Out Who

Level	Elementary onwards
Aims	Getting to know each other; encouraging spoken fluency; practising asking questions; revising simple structures
Duration	20 minutes
Materials	5 blank slips of paper per student
Preparation	1 minute

Procedure

1. Give each student five blank slips of paper.
2. Ask them to write one sentence about themselves on each slip of paper, making five different sentences in total. If necessary, use the board to prompt, eg. *I live ..., I'm ..., I like ...*, etc.
3. Check and help them as they do this.
4. Collect all the slips.
5. Shuffle and redistribute them, giving five to each student again.
6. The task now is for the students to mingle and ask questions, in order to find out who wrote the slips they are holding. They shouldn't show the slips to each other. Prompts for questions may be necessary, eg. *'Do you...?', 'Are you...?'*, etc.
7. Finally, ask the students to report back to the whole class. This will practise the third person forms.

Variations

1. With mixed levels, there is no reason why the students have to produce or be allocated the same number of sentences.
2. You can feed in extra sentences, if you wish, either about yourself or some students, or bogus information. In this way, you can introduce different language items, such as negatives or new vocabulary.

Notes

This activity is in itself a variation of the *Find Someone Who* exercises which are common in activity books, but it avoids photocopying, requires minimal preparation, involves the students in writing, and gives them more freedom and control over the content, while allowing you to dictate the language areas.

Activity 32
Materialistic Matching

Level	Intermediate onwards
Aims	Encouraging oral fluency
Duration	15 minutes
Materials	Magazine photos of people and houses, cars, kitchens, etc.
Preparation	This very much depends! (see Variations and Notes)

Procedure

1. Divide the class into groups of three, four or five.
2. Give each group five photos of people and five of houses (or cars, kitchens, etc.). It isn't necessary for groups to have the same photos.
3. The groups must discuss and agree on a match between the people and the possessions.
4. Each group now presents and justifies their choices to the class, who are free to challenge with questions.

Variations

1. To save preparation time, you can ask students to collect the cuttings at home or during a break, or even devote five minutes of class time to it.
2. Other themes for matching might include dogs, sports, hobbies, films, holidays, favourite dishes or prized possessions.

Notes

Once you have the photos, make sure you keep them for future use.

Activity 33

Senses Dictation

Level	Elementary onwards
Aims	Practising vocabulary; speaking
Duration	15 minutes
Materials	Blank paper
Preparation	None

Procedure

1. Ask the students to prepare a table of five columns, with the following headings: *Hear/See/Feel/Smell/Taste*

2. Dictate a number of words that you want to recycle or use to stimulate discussion, eg. *pink apple goldfish newspaper war scissors wind grammar strawberry sunshine poverty bird limousine* (the name of the place you're in) *ghost museum dog love pollution anger river* (the name of the school you're in) *art mother farm*

3. The students write the words in the column they choose.

4. Invite them to discuss their responses.

Variations

1. Colours can be used as headings, instead of senses.

2. The students can be encouraged to find the student who has the most similar distribution to theirs.

Notes

As with all mismatching activities, the students need to be familiar with the vocabulary first.

Activity 34

Opinion Dictation

Level	Elementary onwards
Aims	Practising writing; speaking
Duration	15 minutes
Materials	Blank paper
Preparation	None

Procedure

1. The students prepare a table, without columns but with these headings:
   - *Strongly agree* on the left
   - *Not sure* in the middle
   - *Strongly disagree* on the right

2. Dictate a number of statements you want to use to stimulate discussion, eg:
   - *Smoking should be allowed in restaurants.*
   - *Fast cars shouldn't be manufactured.*
   - *War will always exist.*
   - *Sports personalities are overpaid.*
   - *Monarchy is an old-fashioned institution.*
   - *Grammar is important.*
   - *Violent films influence viewers.*

3. The students write the sentences on the table where they want, according to the headings. If they strongly agree, they write on the left, etc.

4. Invite them to discuss their responses.

Variation

The students can be encouraged to find the student who has the most similar distribution to theirs.

Notes

The statements can be all about the same topic. This is a good supplementary activity for a coursebook unit.

Activity 35

Fish for It!

Level	Intermediate onwards
Aims	Practising oral fluency
Duration	20 minutes
Materials	Blank paper; a box
Preparation	None

Procedure

1. Ask each student to tear a piece of paper into three strips.
2. They write a statement (about anything) on one slip, a question on another and an exclamation on the third.
3. Collect all the slips and put them, jumbled up, in the box.
4. Ask for two volunteers to sit in front of the class. They will take part in a dialogue together.
5. Elicit from the class two roles for the two volunteers, and a topic for conversation, eg. film director and actor, interview for a part in a new film, etc.
6. The volunteers start the conversation in their roles.
7. When the dialogue begins to falter or the students run out of ideas, one of the class calls out *'Fish!'*
8. When this happens, one of the volunteers picks a slip of paper from the box, and includes it in the dialogue by reading it out.
9. The dialogue must continue as if the new element were quite normal.
10. Change the volunteers, roles and topics as you wish.

Variation

You can give a choice of topics if you want to revise themes you have covered previously.

Notes

It is important to avoid 'forcing' volunteers, as they need to be relaxed enough to be both inventive and spontaneous.

Activity 36

Free Time Pies

Level	Elementary onwards
Aims	Practising the language of routines; hobbies; adverbs of frequency and the present simple tense
Duration	20 minutes
Materials	Blank paper
Preparation	None

Procedure

1. Ask each student to list their hobbies and to order them in terms of frequency.
2. Ask the students to draw a pie diagram, in which the different sectors represent hobbies, and the size of the sector represents the frequency (mathematical precision is not necessary). The students label the sections of the diagram with the names of the activities. Demonstrate yourself first.
3. Each student then writes, on another piece of paper, a few sentences to describe their routines, eg:
   - *I seldom do any gardening.*
   - *I sometimes go to the theatre.*
   - *I have a dance class every week.*
   - *I usually watch the news on TV.*
   - *I always do yoga in the evenings.*
4. Collect the pieces of paper and put them in an accessible place, such as in a box or on a table.
5. Display the pie diagrams around the room.
6. Each student takes a piece of paper and reads it. They have to do two things. Find the matching pie diagram, and find the student who wrote the information. They do the first by circulating and looking at the pie diagrams, and the second by mingling and asking their classmates about their hobbies, eg:
   - *Do you ever do any gardening?*
   - *How often do you go to the theatre?*
   - *When do you do yoga?*
7. They report their findings to the class.

Notes

Make sure they don't write their names on their work until after the activity.

Chapter **3**

Student-generated Activities

Involving learners in the design of their own lessons (and in the design of questionnaires and even tests) provides benefits for both student and teacher. Activity preparation takes place in the learner's time and territory, rather than the teacher's; in fact, the lesson plan is the lesson itself.

1 Student-generated activities

In most classrooms it is the teacher (in most cases aided by the coursebook and the syllabus) who thinks up, designs and administers activities. Student-generated activities, on the other hand, come from the students, for other students (and possibly the teacher!) to do. However, we must assume a certain amount of teacher-dependence in all our students, and it would be unwise to expect them to create their own unprompted activities without guidance. The teacher needs to introduce the concept little by little.

Why should students want to generate their own activities? There are many reasons: it is motivating to challenge other students, it recycles a lot of language, it gives the students more opportunity to be involved in the lesson, it uses personalisation, it allows them to make choices about the language and it encourages them to concentrate on what is useful for them.

Furthermore, it frees the teacher from having to design activities which have more benefit if designed by the students. A teacher might spend two hours preparing an activity which takes the students little time and, more importantly, little linguistic effort to complete, compared to the effort that was needed to go through all the stages of preparation.

Designing a crossword

Here are the steps involved in creating a crossword that will revise the vocabulary of food:

1. Look back at food vocabulary covered.
2. Select words for inclusion in the crossword.
3. Check spellings and meanings.
4. Fit them together into a crossword pattern.
5. Write definitions and other clues.
6. Present everything legibly.

Many teachers may be tempted do all this themselves, and some enjoy doing so. Part of the temptation may be in believing, erroneously, that the students are not capable of doing it. But are there any steps that the student couldn't do, and more importantly, wouldn't derive any linguistic benefit from doing? In other words, the above steps could usefully be included in your lesson plan. Students would make up crosswords for other groups of students, and even the teacher might be challenged into trying to solve one!

It doesn't stop at crosswords. This concept can be applied to a vast range of normal class exercises and games. Almost every exercise you do with your students could be subjected to their creative powers:

- wordsearch
- matching
- spot the error
- pictionary
- snakes and ladders
- odd one out
- gapfills
- charades
- pelmanism

In skills work, students can be encouraged to write their own comprehension questions for their peers to tackle.

The setting up

Teachers will agree that the way an activity is set up can determine to a large extent whether it is successful. Chaos and confusion are counterproductive in even the most fun activity: the activity alone is not enough. Here are some guidelines.

Demonstrate with examples

Avoid asking students to design something they haven't seen before. Don't say *'I'd like you to design a wordsearch for this group'* if they have no idea what a wordsearch is. It's best to start with exercises that are already familiar and, even so, show them an example beforehand.

Get everyone's attention

Signal the need for silence, wait for it, and then use it effectively; this is fundamental to classroom management. As some of the procedures will seem complicated at first, it is crucial that at every stage you have the students' undivided attention.

Give clear instructions
Make them as clear as possible, using demonstrations, gestures, repetitions and comprehension checks where appropriate. If it goes well the first time, you are more likely to be able to repeat it on another occasion, and the smoother it will be. So it is worthwhile taking pains to ensure that the first time is a success.

Make sure everyone knows what to do
As soon as the activity is under way, the teacher's job is to help out where necessary and monitor progress. The first thing is to check that everyone is doing what you asked them to do, in the way you recommended.

The procedure

After showing a sample task, divide the class into groups and explain that the aim is to design a similar task for another group of students. There are four stages, so four groups is ideal. The optimal group size is three students, so you can organise a large class into units of 12 students (the exact number in each group is quite flexible: don't worry about odd numbers). Label the four groups A, B, C and D.

- **Stage 1** is to ask all the groups to design a task. They could all design the same type of task, eg. a crossword, or each group could design a different one (eg. Group A does a crossword, Group B a matching exercise, etc.). They could all work on the same language area, eg. food vocabulary, or each group might work on a different one.
- **Stage 2** involves passing the designed task on to the next group, who have to solve or complete the answers. They can use their notes, confer amongst themselves or you can allow them to ask you. Give them a time limit, but tell them not to worry if they don't finish the task.
- **Stage 3** is to pass it on to the next group, who will correct their performance.
- **Stage 4** takes the task on to the last group, who check everything before handing it back to the original creators.

In this way, the crossword that group A design goes to group B for solving, to group C for correcting and to group D for further checking, before being returned to group A. It is important that all groups see all tasks, because this will maximise the recycling of the language.

Task types and levels

It is important that the students know how to do the tasks before they design their own. Page 45 shows tasks which are usually familiar to students from coursebooks and workbooks. These examples are quite simple, but the level and complexity can be manipulated.

Categorisation task (page 45)
The categories suggested are lexical distinctions associated with travelling. Other categories for one-word examples might be:

- word stress (*stress on 1st syllable/stress on 2nd syllable/stress on other syllable*)
- contrasting vowel or consonant sounds (using phonemic symbols)
- the different prepositions which accompany verbs, nouns, adjectives (*at/of/for/to*)
- verbs followed by *infinitive/gerund/either*
- different ways of forming the past simple (*ed/d/ied/ double consonant/irregular*)
- prefixes used to form opposites (*ir-/il-/un-/im-*)
- the functions of modal verbs (*ability/obligation/ permission*).

But for more extended language practice, the categories could just as easily be:

- preferences (*Things I like doing on holiday/Things I hate doing on holiday*)
- values (*Good advice for tourists here/Bad advice for tourists here*)
- general knowledge (*True/False/Don't know*)
- functions (*Requests/Advice/Asking permission/ Rhetorical questions*)
- conditionals (*0/1st/2nd/3rd/mixed*).

This allows the students to deal with whole sentences rather than individual words, as well as to invest their own opinions and values. Other tasks also lend themselves to such manipulation. You can make tasks easier by adding helpful information, for example in the *Odd One Out* task (page 45), *v* indicates vocabulary, *p* is for pronunciation and *g* is grammar.

Practical implications

Correction
The same procedures apply here as to any activity. If Group B detect an error in Group A's work, they can either ask the teacher about it, refer it back to Group A or correct it themselves, before passing it on to Group C. Or they can ignore it.

Early and late finishers

In a class where the teacher designs and administers all activity, the problem of early finishers comes right back to the teacher, who has to give them something else to do. Here, if Group B solve A's matching exercise quickly, they might be encouraged to add some more questions for C to do. If A can't solve all their task, then B can finish it off when it is passed to them. Also, as there is always something to be done, there is less opportunity for distraction.

Mixed levels

As everybody is involved in the creation of the tasks, they rely on each other and help each other, in order to meet the time deadline. Each is an 'expert' in the task they helped to create, and so weaker students can enjoy a certain amount of authority over stronger peers who need to seek information or clarification.

Peer teaching

It is inevitable that if students are working on materials for each other, then they will be exposed to language from each other, some of which may be new, as students can bring in language learnt outside, as well as inside, the class. This is a useful vehicle for students, motivated by the challenge they are offering others, to slip in new discoveries without showing off, and inter-group communication provides the necessary explanation.

Exploiting the tasks

If the students design beautiful tasks, they can be displayed on the wall. Others might be published in the end-of-course magazine. You could photocopy exercises by one class and give them to another class, and even encourage an inter-class rivalry as they trade tasks. You can surprise them by including their own tasks in their mid-term tests, or keep them in a self-access box or envelope for revision lessons, or for fast finishers in other lessons.

Materials

You need examples of the type of exercises you want the students to design, possibly on OHP transparencies. It also saves time to have blank grids for wordsearch, grouping exercises, etc., ready (see Photocopiable page 46). If you plan to use the technique a lot, you can copy the grids from your original master. It is not efficient, and therefore not recommendable under MINIMAX principles, to have to prepare new grids for every lesson.

The teacher's roles

We have seen that when activity design is transferred from teacher to student, the teacher is freed from much preparation, enabling other roles to be more effectively carried out.

What roles are necessary?

- There must be clear direction, demonstration and explanation, in an atmosphere of control.
- Everyone must be gainfully employed, and this is made easier if everyone knows what to do.
- Help may be solicited and guidance given.
- Students must see a purpose in all this, feel a sense of 'time well spent' and of progress, and that it fits into a scheme.
- They will also appreciate praise for their efforts and feedback on the task, so that if everything doesn't go perfectly, it might have the chance to do so next time.

2 Student-generated questionnaires

Once they have been shown examples (magazines are a good source), students can be encouraged to design their own questionnaires and conduct their own surveys. In this way, the questions are personalised from the imaginations of those setting the questions, and the answers are personalised from the experience, opinions or 'biodata' of the interviewees. With teacher guidance, certain structures, such as conditionals, can be incorporated if appropriate, or certain lexical areas can be targeted. Questions can be of the *Wh-* type or *Yes/No*, or have multi-choice response options. Potential interviewees include student peers, other students in the school, teachers, visitors or complete strangers external to the school, eg. shoppers in an English-speaking environment, or English-speaking tourists. The initial idea might come from the teacher, but the *ideas* come from the students.

Recognising open-ended questions

If students are going to be setting questions for each other, it might be worth guiding them towards the distinction between open and closed questions.

In a text that says *Mr Smith lives in London*, the question *Where does Mr Smith live?* is closed because the answer is factual, comes from a limited choice and can be appraised by an external agent (usually the teacher) who says *'Yes, that's right'*, or offers feedback if the answer is wrong. The answers to closed questions do not generally offer themselves up for prolonged discussion.

However, the question *Would you like to live where Mr Smith lives?* involves just as much research into the text, but adds the opportunity for personalisation. In this case the answer is less factual, opinion-driven, potentially diverse across the class group, open to discussion and closed to correction. Discussion can be extensive. Because of these features, such a question is said to be open-ended. (It is interesting to note that the first question *may* be open-ended if the text does *not* say where Mr Smith lives, in which case each student may speculate individually.)

If students' attention is drawn to this distinction when designing their own activities, they can steer the responses towards or away from discussion as desired. Sometimes a *Yes/No* or factual option is clearer for statistical interpretation, while open-ended questions may reveal a range of response as well as providing more speaking and listening practice.

3 Student-generated tests

It is only one step on from student-generated activities to considering the possibility of having students design their own progress tests. Clearly, I am not including external exams or even internal exams to pass from one level to another. But often teachers and students like to have an informal progress test to see what is understood and remembered. Usually it is the teacher who prepares this, but it is often much better for the students if they take part in informal test design.

Again, consider the steps involved:

- looking back at language covered
- selecting what is felt to be important
- reflecting on typical types of exam task
- considering what constitutes an effective test task
- deciding how much can be answered in the given time
- designing tasks
- ensuring tasks are at the appropriate level
- presenting tasks
- explaining instructions
- allocating marks
- administering the test
- marking the answers
- giving feedback.

Students need to be familiar with all these steps if they are to perform well in external exams, so it is logical to give them practice in designing tests so that they understand them better. There is a danger that tests and exams are held over the heads of students as a sort of mysterious threat or challenge, a strategy made even more unfair if students receive little guidance about the nature of exams and how to pass them. This is similar to writing: there is a danger that something is tested, in the form of homework, for example, before it is even taught (see Chapter 5).

Procedure

When it is time for a progress test, students can work in groups, choose from a list of optional task formats, and design a series of activities for another group. A sample choice is given on page 47 (*Revision Lessons*). Students are encouraged to choose more than one task in more than one topic area, so that the process covers wide revision. This revision procedure could span two lessons: one to design the test, one to do it. Make sure that all work is legible and photocopiable, so that any necessary copies can be made before the next lesson.

Teacher control

The teacher still has a significant measure of control here. You decide when something is to happen, give the choices of task, suggest areas of topics or structures, and advise as to task suitability or level. You can also design tasks for inclusion in the test. You will circulate and make sure that everyone is engaged, knows what to do and is productively working on a realistic and useful activity. If groups finish early, they can be encouraged to choose new tasks to design, but first you might wish to go over their completed designs with them. In other words, you will edit the test, but in class, not at home.

The teacher will offer a choice of tasks, perhaps with a view to familiarising the students with the sort of tasks found in the end-of-year exam or an important external exam relevant to the students. It may be necessary to demonstrate some of the activities before students are required to design their own. In feedback you have the scope to discuss good and bad questions and answers, and consider effective and ineffective strategies. In conclusion, student-generated tests not only help revision, but give effective exam preparation, and therefore do students a great service.

Conclusion

Substantial educational advantage can be obtained from a whole range of class activities and materials that are designed by the students during class, provided that the tasks are set up clearly and that the benefits are made clear to everyone. What may be a routine chore for the teacher can become a challenging research task for the students.

DESIGNED TO PHOTOCOPY

WORDSEARCH

Find 10 words on the subject of CRIME:

P	A	B	C	J	D	E	F
R	O	B	G	U	N	G	H
I	S	L	I	R	J	K	L
S	E	A	I	Y	M	N	O
O	N	C	P	C	E	L	L
N	T	K	L	O	E	T	S
Q	E	M	A	R	S	R	T
U	N	A	W	V	W	I	X
Y	C	I	Y	Z	A	A	B
C	E	L	E	D	E	L	F
G	H	I	R	A	P	E	J

MATCH

hot	wet
dry	hard
strong	cold
soft	weak

accuse	from
prevent	on
congratulate	in
succeed	of

heavy	wind
bitterly	rain
gale force	fog
dense	cold

rough	new
through	now
cough	scuff
bough	scoff

ODD ONE OUT

1 (v)	cat	dog	fish	horse
2 (v)	shoe	tent	house	villa
3 (p)	would	should	mould	good
4 (g)	night	home	work	bed

CATEGORISATION

Put the following words into the categories below:

guide   guide book   flight   museum   nightlife   passport   voyage   travel agent   cruise
cathedral   sun cream   trip   tour   holidaymaker   national park   suitcase   map

PEOPLE	ATTRACTIONS	JOURNEYS	LUGGAGE

DESIGNED TO PHOTOCOPY

WORDSEARCH

Theme: ______________________

Number of words: ______________

MATCH

______________ ______________
______________ ______________
______________ ______________
______________ ______________
______________ ______________
______________ ______________
______________ ______________
______________ ______________
______________ ______________
______________ ______________

ODD ONE OUT

1 (v)	cat	dog	fish	horse
2 (p)	would	should	mould	good
3 (g)	night	home	work	bed
4	______	______	______	______
5	______	______	______	______
6	______	______	______	______
7	______	______	______	______
8	______	______	______	______

CATEGORISATION

Put the following words into the categories below:

DESIGNED TO PHOTOCOPY

Revision Lessons

You are going to prepare a 'test' for another group of students to do.
Please write clearly, preferably in black, so that it may be photocopied.

1 Translations
Translate five English sentences into your mother tongue. Choose sentences which illustrate a language point we have studied, because other students will have to translate them back into English. You can select them from your notes or from the coursebook, or you can make them up.

2 Wordsearch or Crossword
Design your own, with vocabulary we have studied.

3 Categorisation/Grouping task
Jumble up 20 words, to be put into three or four groups. You decide the groups.

4 Gapfill task
Write five sentences, each with one gap, eg. prepositions.

5 Mix 'n' Match task
Choose up to ten pairs, eg. opposites, collocations, verbs + prepositions, and jumble them up.

6 Odd One Out
Produce five lists of four items each. Three of the items in each list will have something in common. One is different.

7 Definitions game
For two words or expressions we have studied, write out three definitions, two of which are wrong.

8 Pictionary
For five words or expressions we have studied, draw pictures which illustrate their meaning.

9 Name three things you can ...
Offer five verbs, eg. *catch* (a cold, a ball, a bus), *spend* (a weekend, a fortune, an hour), *miss* (a person, a target, a film).

10 Spot the Error
Write five sentences, each with one grammatical error.

11 Design a quiz
Ask five factual questions from themes we have studied in the coursebook.

12 Gapfill text
Take a text you have studied. Photocopy it, then use Tipp-ex to blank out up to ten important words.

13 Multiple-choice questions
Write five multi-choice questions on any appropriate topic we have studied, in which three answer-choices are wrong and one is correct. (Alternatively, three are correct and only one is wrong.)

Activity 37

Drawing Loop

Level	Any
Aims	Revising vocabulary
Duration	20 minutes
Materials	Blank paper
Preparation	None

Procedure

1. Divide the class into four groups of three students. In large classes, work in units of 12 students, each unit divided into four groups.
2. Name the groups A, B, C and D.
3. Each group brainstorms and writes a list of about ten words on a given topic, eg. food, rooms, furniture, shops, sports and cities, etc.
4. They all pass their lists on to the next group (A to B, B to C, C to D, D to A).
5. Each group now draws a scene, which must include all the items on the list they have just received. They mustn't label it.
6. They all pass it on, in the same direction as before, to the next group.
7. The groups now label the drawing they have just received.
8. They pass it on. The next group checks the labelling. They correct and complete, where necessary.
9. Finally, the labelled and corrected drawing is passed to the group who wrote the original list.

Variations

1. Brainstorming can be from memory or using coursebooks or notebooks.
2. When the groups label the diagram, they can alternatively write a list of items in the corner, which the next group then has to match to the items drawn.

Notes

1. Make sure that the students write legibly for each other.
2. It works best if they all draw on the same size paper (A4) in the same coloured ink or pencil, especially if you are going to move on to Activity 38 with these drawings, where they will be ideal.
3. It doesn't matter if students can't draw. Ambiguity increases the fun.
4. Try to get all three students drawing together, so that they are all involved in both the activity and the vocabulary recycling.

Activity 38

Quartered Pictures

Level	Any
Aims	Revising vocabulary; practising speaking
Duration	20 minutes
Materials	One picture per four students (see Note)
Preparation	None

Procedure

1. Cut up the pictures into quarters.
2. Divide the class into groups of four students.
3. Shuffle and distribute the quarters. The students mustn't see each other's papers.
4. Tell them that the aim is to find the three other students who have the same picture.
5. They do this by speaking, not showing, so they need to stand up and mingle.
6. When four students think they have the same picture, they tell you, but still without looking at their papers.
7. Check the four papers. If they don't match, tell them to keep mingling.

Notes

1. The drawings from Activity 37 are ideal. A4 size is best.
2. This activity requires the students to know and use the vocabulary of items in the picture, so it is best if they have seen the pictures before.

Activity 39

Word Pancakes

Level	Any
Aims	Revising vocabulary
Duration	20 minutes
Materials	Slips of blank paper (size A8)
Preparation	0-5 minutes (depending on who does it)

Preparation

1. Choose the vocabulary you want to revise.
2. Ask the students to write the words clearly on the slips of paper, one word (or expression) per slip.
3. In a monolingual class, they write the translation on the back of each slip. In a multilingual class, they can write a brief definition or synonym on the back.

Procedure

1. Display the slips, with the target vocabulary face up, on a table.
2. In turn, each student points to one slip and tries to say what is on the reverse of it.
3. If everyone agrees, the same student scoops up the slip, turns it over for everyone to see, and keeps it.
4. If the student is wrong, they turn over the slip to learn the correct answer, but leave it as it was on the table.
5. The student with the most slips is the winner.
6. Repeat the activity (at some point), but with the target vocabulary face down, to test recall.

Variations

1. Ask the students which words *they* would like to include.
2. The task in the activity can vary according to level, eg. it could be to make a sentence using the word.

Notes

1. The students could prepare the slips themselves. Cutting one A4 sheet into 16 slips only takes a moment. You need one slip for every word of vocabulary.
2. In large classes, divide the class into groups of about eight or ten students. In this case, you will need enough slips to cover the same vocabulary in each group.
3. This activity needn't end. It can be ongoing, as new vocabulary is added and recycled alongside the familiar words.
4. Keep the slips for future use. They are of negligible weight and volume!
5. These slips can be used for many other activities. You might like to choose from the following activities:

Drawing Quiz

Procedure

1. Mix up the slips of paper, and put them into a box or bag.
2. One student picks out one slip of paper.
3. The student has to draw a picture illustrating the meaning of the vocabulary on the slip.
4. The rest of the class guess the word or expression.

Variation

This can be done in teams. Each student draws for their own team to guess. The team is timed, and the quickest team is the winner.

Storytelling Game

Procedure

1. Divide the class into groups of three or four students.
2. Each team selects five slips at random.
3. They make up a story, which includes those five words or expressions.
4. They tell their stories to the class.
5. The listeners have to say which five items were used in the story.

(continued on next page)

Variations

1. This can be made into a competition, with each team winning points for each item they identify correctly.
2. The identification can wait until the end, once all the stories have been told.

Test Each Other

Procedure

1. Give a number of slips to students, sitting in pairs.
2. They test each other. One has the slip, and reads out the translation or definition, and the other says the target vocabulary. Then they exchange roles.

Notes (for all three activities)

1. Make sure all the students participate, if possible.
2. Drawing competence is irrelevant. Ambiguity adds to the enjoyment.
3. Linking words or expressions are arguably as important as nouns and verbs. Add these to the collection.
4. The task of identifying items provides a reason to listen.
5. Frequent testing is useful, challenging and fun. It gives a sense of progress and is easy to organise.

Activity 40

Headline News

Level	Intermediate onwards
Aims	Practising writing
Duration	30 minutes
Materials	News photographs; blank paper
Preparation	None (if you already have the photos)

Procedure

1. Arrange the students in groups of three or four.
2. Give each group a photo, and ask them to create a headline to go with it. You might like to demonstrate the process first.
3. These are then displayed around the room.
4. Ask the students to circulate and look at the photos with the headlines.
5. They write questions about the stories according to their own curiosity.
6. The original group then takes the photo, headline and questions and writes an article, making sure all the questions are answered.
7. Display the finished articles, so that the whole class can circulate and read them. They can check if their questions have been answered.

Variations

1. They can choose their own photo.
2. You can also give out authentic headlines, which the students can match with a photo.

Notes

1. Some exposure to newspapers and their written style would be appropriate before this activity.
2. To encourage students to write questions, add your own as you circulate.
3. If students write their own questions, this will provide an extra reason to read the finished article.

Activity 41
Question These Answers!

Level	Elementary onwards
Aims	Practising questions
Duration	15 minutes
Materials	Blank paper
Preparation	None

Procedure

1. Elicit some information about a given topic, such as 'the UK'. Contributions might include:
   Oasis red Hugh Grant whisky St Paul's Cardiff Wembley Boxing Day St Patrick Prince Charles Big Ben Damien Hirst tea
2. Write these on the board.
3. Divide the class into groups.
4. Each group has to write as many questions as possible, but the answers must be from the list of words on the board.
5. Collect the questions. Rub the answers off the board.
6. Rearrange the students, so that at least one member of each of the previous groups is in each new group.
7. Name the students in each group A, B, C, D, etc.
8. Choose a question at random. Read it out. Allow a 'conference stage', when students can exchange information.
9. Call out a student from one group to answer. If correct, they get one point. If not, ask a student with the corresponding letter in another group.

Variation

Rather than eliciting, you could dictate or write the information on the board.

Notes

1. Seeing the 'answers' first helps less confident students choose or understand how to answer correctly.
2. The 'conference stage' enables weaker students, who know the answer, to help stronger ones who don't.

Activity 42
Quiz Reconstruction

Level	Elementary onwards
Aims	Practising question formation
Duration	20 minutes
Materials	Blank paper; a few quiz questions
Preparation	5 minutes

Procedure

1. Divide the class into two or more teams and ask about six questions, eg:
   - *What has feathers, sings, builds a nest and can fly?*
   - *What is long, thin and legless with a poisonous bite?*
   - *What barks and lives in a kennel?*
   - *What has shoes, a mane and a tail?*
   - *What has eight legs and builds a web?*
   - *What swims and has scales but no legs ?*
2. Go over the answers.
3. Ask the groups to try to remember the questions. Go over the answers.
4. Now ask the groups to recreate the original questions.
5. They read their questions out in turn to the other team(s), who must answer them.
6. Go over all the answers, allowing the students to give feedback on their own answers.

Variations

1. Types of question can vary enormously, eg:
   Passives: *What was discovered by Columbus?*
   Relative clauses: *Name the place where rockets are launched in Florida.*
2. Formats also vary a great deal. Some have multiple-choice answers, eg:
   Second conditional:
   What would you do if ...?
   Would you: a) ... b) ... c) ... d) ...?

Notes

The challenge of productive language lies in the reconstruction and design of quizzes. Otherwise they are largely receptive, simply test general knowledge, and *you* do all the work.

Activity 43

Two Lesson Bridge

Level	Elementary onwards
Aims	Helping to listen to cassettes; practising questions; practising reading
Duration	20 minutes in two lessons
Materials	Cassette recording; copies of its tapescript for each group
Preparation	2 minutes (to photocopy the tapescript)

Procedure

1 Lesson One: Divide the class into groups of four.

2 Give each group a copy of the tapescript.

3 They read it and write questions, to test another group's comprehension of the text. They should make a note of the answers.

4 Collect the questions.

5 Lesson Two: Introduce the listening activity and hand out the sheets of questions. Rotate the question sheets so that no group has the questions they designed.

6 Play the cassette and ask the students to answer the questions.

7 Afterwards, each group reads out the questions they answered, together with their answers.

8 The group who set the questions gives feedback on the answers.

Variation

You can determine the number of questions the groups must ask, if you wish.

Notes

1 When they come to listen in the second lesson, the students are familiar with the text's content, which will help the task of listening. However, the text won't have been heard, and the questions will be unseen.

2 There is a chance that weaker students will be an authority over stronger ones as they give feedback on students' answers to their group's questions, even if they didn't design all the questions themselves.

Activity 44

Multi-Choice Dictation

Level	Intermediate onwards
Aims	Getting to know each other more; revising conditionals
Duration	20 minutes
Materials	Nine sentences about the teacher, six of which are false
Preparation	10 minutes (to prepare the dictation)

Procedure

1 Read out the first three sentences of your dictation. The students only write one, the one they think is true for you.

2 Continue the dictation, reading the sentences in groups of three. It might be something like this:

1 a) *If I want entertainment I watch TV.*
  b) *I prefer to see live music if possible.*
  c) *I'm happiest when I'm alone.*

2 a) *I'll move to China next year if I get a job there.*
  b) *I might stay here if I'm lucky.*
  c) *I'll probably give up teaching if I find a better paid job.*

3 a) *If I could be someone else I'd be a rock star.*
  b) *If I was rich I'd become a novelist.*
  c) *If I had the space I'd buy a grand piano.*

3 Go over the answers, allowing discussion where appropriate.

4 Encourage the students to design their own similar dictation exercise.

5 Divide them into groups of three or four. They take it in turns to dictate to the other group members.

6 They discuss the answers.

Variation

This can be used for any structure.

Notes

This activity personalises the structures, but at the same time requires accuracy.

Activity 45
True/False Dictation

Level	Elementary onwards
Aims	Practising any structure; practising listening, writing and speaking
Duration	15 minutes
Materials	Blank paper
Preparation	10 minutes

Procedure

1. Prepare some sentences for the students to consider, and which practise the desired structure. Here, it is 'verbs followed by the infinitive or *-ing* form', eg:
   - *I remember learning to swim.*
   - *I never forget to do my homework.*
   - *I often stop studying to have cups of coffee.*
   - *I like to visit the dentist twice a year.*
   - *I enjoy going to school.*
2. Dictate the sentences.
3. If a sentence is true for the student, they write the sentence.
4. If the sentence isn't true, they must write a related sentence that *is* true, eg. *I can't remember learning to swim.*
5. Finally, encourage the students to share and discuss their responses.

Variations

1. The students can find someone who has the most similar responses to theirs.
2. This activity can be used for any structure (and therefore any level).

Note

This activity personalises the structures, but at the same time requires accuracy.

Activity 46
Switcheroo Dialogues

Level	Elementary onwards
Aims	Practising reading and writing dialogues
Duration	15 minutes
Materials	Blank paper
Preparation	None

Procedure

1. The students sit in a circle or, in a large class, several circles.
2. Everyone needs a blank piece of paper.
3. They each choose a dialogue situation (from a selection you give, if you wish) and write the theme at the top of the page.
4. Every student initiates a dialogue, writing the first exchange on the first line.
5. The paper is passed on to the student on the left.
6. Every student now responds to the dialogue in front of them, by writing an appropriate reply or exchange.
7. The papers are passed back to the right, so that everyone receives the dialogue they started.
8. The conversation is built up by passing to and fro between the same two writers.
9. An apt conclusion is for the pairs to read out their dialogues to the class.

Variation

The dialogues could be constructed by passing them round the circle, with a different writer for each line. This gives more reason to listen when they are read out, as more writers are involved.

Activity 47

Photo Dialogues

Level	Elementary onwards
Aims	Practising reading; writing dialogues
Duration	20-30 minutes
Materials	One photo of couples for each pair of students (see Note 1)
Preparation	None (if you already have the photos)

Procedure

1. Number the photos and pin them up around the classroom.
2. In pairs, the students circulate, look at the photos and choose one, without removing it.
3. Each pair writes a dialogue of eight to ten lines, based on the photo, but avoiding obvious reference to the characters, eg. they shouldn't name the people in the photo. The students write their names at the top of their dialogues.
4. The completed dialogues are pooled, jumbled and put in an accessible place.
5. Each pair now comes and chooses a dialogue, reads it, then walks round trying to find the relevant photo.
6. When they have guessed the photo, they write their names at the bottom of the dialogue alongside the photo number.
7. They return the dialogue to the pool and pick up another one to work with.
8. Every pair writes their names and the photo number they have guessed at the bottom of each dialogue.
9. The dialogues are returned to those who wrote them, who judge the winners from the list at the bottom.

Variation

If you prefer not to have the students moving around, or cannot do that, you can ask them to choose a photo and work on it in pairs privately. Later, you can display the photos at the front of class, and distribute the dialogues for matching.

Notes

1. The photos should all contain two people or, for humorous effect, animals, etc.
2. You can direct the content of the activity if you wish, specifying topics you want the students to practise, eg. functions such as *asking a favour*, etc.
3. Encourage the students to write legibly.
4. You can include your own dialogues in the pool, feeding in target language.
5. Fast finishers can read or write more dialogues, lengthen them or be given further dialogues written by the teacher or by other classes.

Chapter **4**

Exploiting Materials

Whether you or your students prepare material yourself, or find authentic sources, everything can be kept for other lessons, for other purposes, for other levels. Adapt it and make the most of it. And there are many ways of making the most of your coursebook without having recourse to hours of preparation and mountains of photocopies.

The coursebook

As teachers, we often ask how we can make the coursebook lesson more interesting, supplementing or even replacing it with new ideas and materials. However, there is a danger that more photocopies are made, students wonder why they bought the book, the lesson may end up more disjointed, and we may find that what is interesting or dull for one person may not be so for others.

It is worth making the effort to photocopy less. The coursebook is already full of reading matter, and photocopying usually means more. Also, students are passive recipients of photocopies, with the teacher once again robbing them of participation in their learning: they could easily be activated by being asked to copy something by hand (within reason, of course!). Loose photocopies are difficult to organise and easily lost, and more paper doesn't necessarily lead to increased learning. Furthermore, photocopying is unecological, expensive, stressful at times (especially if left until just before the lesson) and quite possibly illegal.

Coursebook writers have already done the hard work for us, and while teachers frequently complain about some aspects of coursebooks, there are usually plenty of plus-points worth exploiting in each book. Given the potential for haphazard syllabus planning and erratic teaching without them, coursebooks and workbooks are probably the best set of notes the students take away.

Interesting lessons can be coursebook-based, although merely following the book step by step can be dry. What is needed is to bring the book to life, and to remember that learning comes from challenge, involvement, fun, variety, personal investment and hard work - on the part of the students!

Getting to know the coursebook

A quiz can help students to orientate themselves through the book and show them how the book can help them. The questions will differ according to the book, but once designed, keep the quiz for further use. It needn't be photocopied; it can be dictated, projected on an OHP or pinned on the wall for the students to find. Personalised questions encourage student-generated activities right from the start: in fact most, if not all, of the quiz could be written by opposing teams.

On the very first day a new class can be divided into competing teams in a brief coursebook quiz such as the following:

Coursebook Quiz (time limit five minutes)

1. What's the name of Unit 11, and what is it about?
2. What do you find at the end of each unit?
3. Is it possible to read what you hear on the cassette? Where?
4. On which page is there a photo of a pop star?
5. There is a story in Unit 10. Which country is it set in?
6. Are there any exercises to help your writing? Give a page number.
7. Which unit is about driving and transport?
8. Which unit covers reported speech?
9. What pronunciation features are covered in Unit 3?
10. Are there any songs in the book? Where?
11. Your own question
12. Your own question

Quiz the students regularly on the factual content of the coursebook, from the population of the city described in Unit X to the colour of the man's hair on page Y or the time that Mrs Z gets up in the morning.

If you test students on their memories frequently, by means of informal quizzes about lists, collocations, language rules, photograph contents, etc., this will challenge them in an enjoyable and motivating way.

Changing the medium

Apart from the 'visuals' and recorded material, most of the coursebook contents are in the medium of black print on white paper, intended for reading. To add extra interest and make them more memorable, the contents can be displayed in a variety of media. Not only will this add variety, but it will give a broader coverage to cater for diverse learning styles (see Chapter 6), increasing the potential across the class.

Use different colours on the whiteboard or blackboard to appeal to visually/spatially oriented students, or display text on the wall to encourage physical participation, such as circulating around the room. The text is still that of the coursebook, but the classroom dynamic produces more interest than merely reading from the book.

Put the content onto cards or slips of paper (Activities 48-50), to be dictated instead of read. Vocabulary can be drawn rather than written, and realia can be handled by those kinesthetic learners!

Using the visuals

Rather than hunt around for flashcards, the photographs and diagrams in the coursebook can be used in a number of useful and entertaining ways.

Every photo must illustrate at least ten vocabulary items in a visual context. This can be capitalised upon by memory and search-and-find activities:

- One student lists the items in a photo, or describes it, and the rest of the class have to find it. Or the students have to write down 10 things in a photo, then it becomes a competition to see who can say their list by heart.
- The teacher shows a photo in a quick flash or a slow reveal to encourage guessing, which might provide a good lead in to the subject matter, as well as involving the students in recall and production.
- Students can choose and compare two pictures, one they like and one they don't.

Visuals can be further exploited by hypothesising, roleplaying and speculating. Students can put themselves in the position of the people in the picture and act out the situation, taking on a new mood or persona. They can make up 'what if' situations (eg. *What if the people in the photo had an argument and fell out, what would it be about, and who would take which view?*), guess what may have happened before or predict what might happen after the photo was taken.

Using the texts

Prediction plays an important role in linking printed texts with the learner's imagination. A title is enough to start the reader thinking about the rest of the text, so this is worth exploiting.

Ask the students to predict the content from the title alone. With a few key words from the text, the students can even make up their own brief story. This will give them a reference with which to compare the targeted text, and will also preview some vocabulary without intimidating the students.

Very often we pre-teach vocabulary unnecessarily. This is because we assume that they don't know an item because we haven't explicitly taught it to them ourselves. But we can't know what the students don't know until they tell us and, anyway, the context of the text is probably the clearest presentation for the vocabulary. It might be more efficient to ask the students to tell us what the text means after reading it than to spend time 'teaching' words out of context because of an assumption that our students won't be able to cope.

Students can be encouraged to write their own comprehension questions for each other. Don't forget that opinions are also useful topics for questions and lead more naturally into discussion. Their own questions can be used for a quiz in which students collaborate for answers, and the weaker students can often be found helping the stronger ones (see Chapter 6). Finally, the texts in the coursebook can be used for projects and simulations.

Exploiting the vocabulary

Linking with ideas described earlier in this book, vocabulary can be reinforced by means of personalisation (Activity 25) and open-ended activities (see Chapter 2), using memory games (Activity 24), and through student-generated activities (see Chapter 3).

Developing the themes

The different themes or topics can be a useful source of discussion. As a revision exercise, students could be asked to talk about particular themes picked at random, using the book as a guide. They could do this while playing a board game, landing on topics covered in the course. An alternative is to ask students in pairs to agree on the five most useful or interesting themes covered. Then the pairs are combined and the foursome has to agree on the same list of five themes. This continues as a Pyramid Debate until everyone agrees (Activity 15).

Disguising the exercises

Between the coursebook and the workbook there is usually a wealth of good practice exercises. A motivating way to steadily progress through about six of these in half an hour is to disguise them with a competition. Draw a racetrack on the board and divide the students into teams, each with a coloured car (or horse, boat, snail, etc.). As the teams successfully complete each exercise, they move around the racetrack. Imaginary prize money can be won for perfectly correct exercises.

A more elaborately disguised race circuit involves drawing a landscape of a mountain, lake, snakepit and castle, over which teams move if they complete certain exercises. For example, their team gets to the top of the mountain if they get over half of Exercise 1 correct, winning a bonus set of skis if they get over 80% right. This continues for the next five exercises down the mountain, into the lake, out of the lake, over the snakepit and up the hill to the castle, winning aqualungs, harpoon guns, rope and sovereigns as bonuses to help them on the journey. Finally, at the castle, they can exchange their bonuses for imaginary cash. This makes an adventure out of simple workbook drill exercises.

Noughts and Crosses is another useful game for distracting students' attention from the language work they are practising (Activity 51). Finally, an effective and absorbing game which practises or even presents grammar structures is *Sentence Hangman*, far more sophisticated than its one-word ancestor (Activity 52).

Authentic materials

While photocopying may need copyright permission, authentic originals may be used in class and cut up freely. They provide a rich source of reading material and the visuals such as photographs, cartoons and games can all be exploited.

Photographs

Photographs offer fresh, up-to-date, often amusing or curious images, and students may be more interested in current events and famous people than the possibly outdated ones in the coursebook. It is worth building up a stock of photos, and the students may be encouraged to collect them themselves.

Here are some suggested categories to collect:

- adverts
- individuals
- clothes
- objects
- houses
- famous people
- current affairs
- couples/groups of people
- postures
- landscapes/places
- vehicles
- food
- sports
- surreal, striking or unusual images

And here are some suggestions for using them:

- Encourage students to categorise the pictures themselves.
- Study the vocabulary of any topic.
- Play *Happy Families* (Activity 76).
- Memorise the contents of pictures.
- Describe the picture for later identification.
- Spot the difference between similar pictures.
- Put pictures in order of preference or according to a narrative.
- Make up a story from a given picture.
- Write a reaction to the picture (Activity 53).
- Write a dialogue for the picture (Activity 47).
- Identify unusual angles or surreal images.
- Practise grammar structures (eg. *is doing/is going to do/has just done*).
- Match the picture to an advertising slogan or product.

The ideal collection has pictures which lend themselves to numerous uses. For example, photos of people can be used for physical description, clothes, actions, locations, narratives, dialogues, speculation and role-play.

Authentic sources

Some newspapers are local and therefore of immediate relevance to the students. An English publication about what's going on in their own city may be very motivating, especially for news and cultural events, including concerts, theatre and cinema. Encourage students to look out for these themselves. The internet is an obvious source which students are likely to browse through independently.

The following can be done with just one or two publications:

- Practise reading authentic texts.
- Speculate as to type of reader.
- Compare the layout, content and style of different newspapers.
- Match the story with a headline or photo (Activity 40).
- Read and answer letters.
- Study the grammar and other language items.
- Compare the same story or review in different newspapers.
- Study adverts.
- Look for examples of wordplay and humour.
- Arrange current affairs debates.
- Write a reaction to an article (Activity 53).
- Study the language of headlines.
- Research into current affairs.
- Study political bias, 'reading between the lines' and euphemism.

The students' own work

The students produce a wealth of material during a course, some of which may be interesting reading, and most of which is language output. Whatever they feel about their work, they will feel better if you show an interest in it, and give the impression that others might benefit from reading it. Students may be reluctant about showing their work to others, so this issue requires delicacy, but reluctance often comes from insecurity, in that the students don't feel that their work is of any use, rather than from a desire to be secretive. What can be done with the students' own work? Here are a few suggestions:

Show it to new classes as examples
There is some logic in referring to students' work, because it shows measures of improvement. If you are teaching letter-writing skills, examples of letters illustrating those skills are of great use: it is definitely worth collecting them.

Display it on the wall
Students can circulate freely and read. This contributes to the notion of immersion of the learners in English.

Collect errors for later treatment
There is plenty of lesson material here. If you collect errors, both seen and heard, you can put them together into a list for students to correct themselves. This can be a team game, to decide which sentences are incorrect and to correct them. Lists of errors can be kept in the self-access box, too.

Encourage replies and reactions
If students read each other's texts, they can write messages to the authors, asking questions or commenting. This can start an exchange similar to that of *Dear Object* (Activity 63). If students have email, it can be exploited to practise written communication amongst the class, out of class, at home or in the computer room or self-access centre.

Ask students to edit it for a magazine
This is an excellent end for any piece of student output. It is then displayed, circulated and taken home, and possibly read many times.

Encourage critical appraisal/feedback amongst students
Also requiring sensitivity, this practice can help students to improve their skills: they get used to looking for errors or appraising style, and this will rub off on their own production. The author, too, benefits from hearing opinions from different perspectives.

Create tasks from student texts
With the students' permission, you may take a finished piece of work and design a task around it. And the task might be to encourage the students to design a task around it.

Use student-generated materials for revision
The students may be engaged in preparing cards, worksheets or other materials (see Chapter 3 and Activities 39 and 48). These materials can be stored in the self-access box for later use or for when it is time for revision.

Conclusion

Probably in every staffroom in the world, however well-resourced, some teachers are busily reinventing the wheel by creating their own materials when the same thing is already on the shelf. It may seem the quickest option, but a more efficient approach is to take the trouble to check through all resources available to you at the start. Remember that the most useful of these may well be the coursebook, and a skilled teacher will exploit this to the full, both to cut down preparation and to serve the students better.

Activity 48

Loop Card Transformations

Level	Intermediate onwards (Cambridge examination students in particular)
Aims	Practising common structures; developing oral accuracy; changing a writing activity into an oral one
Duration	10-20 minutes
Materials	20 cards (per 20 students)
Preparation	20 minutes (the first time you do the activity only)

Transformations are pairs of sentences, and the objective is to complete the second sentence so that it means the same as the first. They are common in coursebooks, especially those preparing candidates for Cambridge examinations, eg:

1a
It was such awful weather that I didn't go on the excursion.
1b
The weather ...

2a
'I won't be late,' she said to her client.
2b
She told ...

3a
Snow covered the little village in the valley.
3b
The little village ...

Preparation

Before the lesson, copy sentence 1a onto your first card. At the bottom of the card put the beginning of sentence 1b. Number the card **1a**. Card 1a looks like this:

> **1a**
> It was such awful weather that I didn't go on the excursion.
> The weather ...

Write the answer for Card 1a on your second card, include a sentence beginning which leads to the original sentence of 1a, and number this second card **1b**. Card 1b looks like this:

> **1b**
> The weather was so awful that I didn't go on the excursion.
> It was ...

Continue this process for the remaining transformations. Transformations often come in exercises of ten, which is why you need 20 cards.

Procedure

1. Keep the cards in their pairs and place them on a chair in front of the class.
2. The students work in pairs, Student A and Student B.
3. Explain by demonstration.
4. Each pair of students takes one pair of cards. They take one card each, and mustn't look at each other's.
5. Student A reads sentence 1a silently and has to try and say 1b correctly. Student B listens and prompts until Student A can say it perfectly.
6. Student B does the same for sentence 1a, prompted by student A, who can see it.
7. When they have finished that particular pair of transformations, they return the two cards to the chair and select another pair.

Variations

In some transformations, a prompt is given, which must be used in the answer:

1a
It was such awful weather that I didn't go on the excursion.
1b
(so)

The cards could give this prompt instead of a sentence beginning, so that Card 1a would look like this:

> **1a**
> It was such awful weather that I didn't go on the excursion.
> (so)

(continued on next page)

Card 1b would look like this:

1b The weather was so awful that I didn't go on the excursion. (such)

Notes

1. This activity turns transformations from written into oral practice, involving memory retention and automatisation of target structures.
2. The true MINIMAX value here lies in the students' creating their own cards once they know the technique.
3. It is also useful in classes of mixed levels, as the students can work at their own speed. Early finishers can start writing the cards for another exercise.
4. Finally, the written exercise in the book can be given for homework.

Activity 49

Bold Statements

Level	Intermediate onwards
Aims	Encouraging oral fluency; recycling language from the coursebook
Duration	20 minutes
Materials	One slip of paper or card per student
Preparation	5 minutes

Procedure

1. Write out bold or contentious statements on slips of paper or card, one statement per card. You need one card per student. You can base them on the coursebook theme you are currently teaching, eg. for the theme of travel:
   - *It is better to travel light and alone.*
   - *Hitchhiking is extremely dangerous.*
   - *I prefer a beach holiday.*
   - *I would enjoy a holiday in space.*
   - *Campsites are better than hotels.*
2. Allow the students to choose one slip and give them some time to think.
3. Each student has to talk about the statement, interpreting its meaning and giving their own opinion.
4. Other students offer their comments.

Variations

1. You might like to demonstrate first, by picking a card yourself and talking about it.
2. You can add a competitive element, by asking the other students to predict whether the speaker will agree or disagree with the statement (once they've heard what it is).
3. As with any discussion, work can be included on reported speech, focusing on each card for revision, eg. *Judit thought that hitchhiking could be dangerous, and she said she wouldn't like to do it.*
4. Students, once familiar with the activity, can generate their own Bold Statements.

Notes

Don't forget to keep the cards. They will provide a useful filler for another day.

Activity 50

Ask Around

Level	Intermediate onwards
Aims	Encouraging oral fluency; recycling language from the coursebook
Duration	20-30 minutes
Materials	One slip of paper or card per student
Preparation	5 minutes

Procedure

1. Write out questions on slips of paper or card, one statement per card. You can invent them, based on the coursebook theme you are currently teaching, or you might take them directly from the coursebook, eg. for the theme of marriage:
    - *Do you believe in arranged marriages?*
    - *Would you sign a pre-nuptial contract?*
    - *Is marriage out of date?*
    - *Do people get married too early or too late?*
    - *Is divorce too easy nowadays?*
2. Ask the students to choose one slip.
3. Each student has to ask their question to as many other students as possible, recording the general results, eg. *15 said yes and 12 said no.*
4. They all report back to the class about the results.

Variations

1. You may wish to demonstrate first by picking a card yourself and asking students about it.
2. As with any discussion, work can be included on reported speech, eg. *Eszter said that she wouldn't sign a pre-nuptial contract because ...*
3. For higher levels, indirect questions can be demanded.
4. Students, once familiar with the activity, can generate their own questions.

Notes

1. You may need to teach or revise terms such as *three-quarters of the class, 50%, 19 out of 24 students*, etc.
2. Remember to keep the cards. They will provide a useful filler for another day.

Activity 51

Noughts and Crosses Grammar

Level	Intermediate onwards
Aims	Practising any structure. Here, it is reported speech.
Duration	15 minutes
Materials	None
Preparation	None

Procedure

1. Draw the Noughts and Crosses grid on the board:

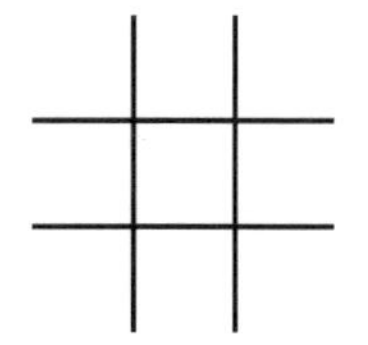

2. Write in it nine reporting verbs, one in each space, eg. *asked, advised, suggested, promised, apologised, insisted, denied, admitted, told.*
3. Divide the class into two teams and decide who will start.
4. The first team selects a verb, and has to produce a correct sentence with it.
5. If it is correct, they win the square in which the verb is written.
6. The objective is to get three squares in a row – horizontally, vertically or diagonally.

Variations

1. You can play this with innumerable structures.
2. You might like to help the students with a choice of options in this structure. Give them a list, eg:
    - *he ... me to do*
    - *she ... that I should do*
    - *he ... doing*
    - *she ... if I would do*
    - *he ... on doing*
    - *she ... to do*
    - *he ... for doing*
    - *she ... me that ...*

Activity 52

Sentence Hangman

Level	Elementary onwards
Aims	Practising any structure. Here, it is the third conditional.
Duration	15 minutes
Materials	None
Preparation	None

Procedure

1. Think of a full sentence containing a structure you would like to present or revise.
2. Write it on the board, using bars instead of letters, eg:

   -- -'- -----, -'- ---- ---- ---.

   This represents *If I'd known, I'd have told you.*
3. Divide the class into two teams and decide who will start.
4. Each team says one letter or one word.
5. If the letter is in the sentence, they get one point for every time it appears. Write it in the correct spaces. If the letter is not in the sentence, they lose a point.
6. If they guess a word correctly, they get five points, but they lose five points if it isn't correct.
7. Continue until the students have discovered the sentence. Add up the points.

Variation

This activity works with any structure.

Notes

You can present new structures with this, but it might help to give a context for the sentence beforehand, eg. the end of a story, or the punchline of a joke.

Activity 53

Cutting Comments

Level	Intermediate onwards
Aims	Practising reading and writing
Duration	20-30 minutes
Materials	Several short news articles or cuttings; blank paper
Preparation	None (if you have the cuttings ready)

Procedure

1. Display the cuttings around the class, on any available surface. Put a piece of blank paper beside each photo.
2. Invite the students to circulate slowly and read all the articles, starting anywhere. They stop and write a comment on every piece of paper that accompanies the cutting.
3. Divide the class into the same number of groups as there are articles.
4. Distribute one article and the accompanying comments sheet to each group. Allow them to choose, if this is practical.
5. The group have to construct a written summary of the comments on each article. They can choose how to do this, eg. it can be an article, review, poem, interview, dialogue, story or a simple report.

Variations

1. This activity works equally well using photographs rather than cuttings of texts. Obscure or unusual images may provide more scope for the imagination, but photos of people offer plenty of potential. The photos can be cut from magazines, etc.
2. In large classes, instead of the students circulating round the room, you might prefer to divide them into groups first and give each group a collection of articles. They can pass them round and add their comments.

Notes

Once you have the cuttings, keep them for future use.

Chapter 5

Inspiring Writing

The skill of writing is frequently left as a homework task without the necessary encouragement, preparation or training. Yet writing can be introduced in class in imaginative ways, often linked to other skills, particularly reading.

Writing as a class activity

Writing is important because it practises and consolidates language, and at the same time creates permanent records. These records, like photographs, show 'frozen' points in progressive language development. Writing forces students to concentrate on accuracy, but errors are not inhibiting as they might be in oral communication. It is an intrapersonal (see Chapter 6), reflective activity, which involves language revision, thought and the risk-taking processes necessary for progress. All writing is creative, although some is artistic, some is functional, and some is both. The distinction is not important here, as both can communicate effectively and arouse a sense of pride in the finished product. The two can develop together, to mutual benefit, and need not be treated as separate fields as far as the students are concerned.

The temptation to give writing as a homework task is understandable: it takes time, is often an individual activity, and it may seem dull compared to other classroom activities. But writing skills don't materialise out of thin air, even if inspiration might, so even homework tasks need preparation in class. Writing can be an enjoyable and dynamic classroom activity, with the minimum of preparation time and materials.

Reading and writing

Writing should not be too divorced from reading, as often the stimulus for writing comes from something we have read. Job applications and letters of complaints usually respond to advertisements, emails provoke replies, and letters between friends alternate responses. Also, sample texts are useful for illustrating appropriate expressions and writing conventions in the same way that reading stories inspires authors to write them. The students' own writing can be used as a stimulus for other students to write in response and, because it is personalised, it becomes an absorbing activity.

One valuable activity is to exchange letters with your students. Your letters needn't be long and can be prepared on a word processor, kept on file and used with several classes after only minor changes, if any. You can feed in new language in context and reinforce language that you have covered in class. The students learn the conventions of informal letter writing informally, and the activity involves authentic, personalised communication. Their replies will come from a mixture of the language they have studied in class, the language input of your letter and the desire to respond to your communication. All this leads the students into experimenting with language, and their letter writing may well improve dramatically in a very short space of time.

From reception to production

In terms of developing writing skills, activities can be thought of as following a cline, or gradient, from reception to production. The whole spectrum need not be covered in a rigid programme, but it helps to remember how difficult it is to write in a vacuum devoid of inspiration, input or purpose.

PRODUCTION
Writing freely
Writing from non-textual stimuli
Responding to written texts
Writing according to constraints
Copycat writing
Changing the interpretation
Writing from written prompts
Being creative with existing texts
Reacting to written texts
RECEPTION

Reacting to written texts
The students are given texts and react to them in 'non-written' forms, such as interpreting and discussing them, drawing a picture inspired by the text (Activities 54-55)

or reading the text aloud, perhaps in creative or unusual ways. The teacher may use dictation, which can be extremely varied, linguistically challenging and also useful for calming things down in a boisterous class (Activities 44-45).

Being creative with existing texts
Going one step along the gradient, texts which have already been written are changed and reformulated. This must be done with sensitivity (Activity 56).

Writing from written prompts
The use of written prompts helps the students to focus on the content at sentence level, without worrying about the structure and direction of the whole text (Activities 57-58).

Changing the interpretation
Writing is artistically satisfying only if the reader interprets it as such, and interpretations can change in the light of a new perspective. Activities 26 and 59 involve such changes in perspective, which give new meaning to an initially straightforward exercise.

Copycat writing
This involves copying only the format of something that is already written. In the case of a song or poem, the metre and rhyme scheme may be kept, but the students change the words and theme. Limericks and 'haiku' are variations of the same idea, as these poems always have the same length and format (including rhyme, in the case of limericks). All you need is an example to show the students, which might be a copy of your favourite song or poem. Examine the structure of it together and then encourage the students to change the words while keeping the same structure.

Writing according to constraints
Curiously enough, it is easier to write according to strict constraints than it is to write freely. One reason is that you can blame the constraints for making it difficult, feeling proud of what you have written 'despite' them (Activities 60-62).

Responding to written texts
Coursebooks frequently present examples of written texts (such as letters), encourage study of the example, and set tasks in response. The text presented may have useful language which the students can practise in their replies, and thinking up content for a piece of writing is no longer a problem, as that is decided by the task.

Reading can serve as a springboard for written comment, and individual students' reactions can help to provide the content for the task of writing a summary. Starting off with newspaper cuttings can provide authenticity, and other students' comments provide personalisation (Activity 53).

But there is no need to search far for written input on which to comment: it can come from the students themselves (Activities 20, 64-65). You can get the students sitting in a circle and passing written contributions on, such as in *Switcheroo Dialogues*, where dialogues are written by two students, each responding to the other (Activity 46). The written output develops from the interplay between the students' imaginations, while the teacher may feed in language as required.

Such activities are frequently collaborative: for example, building up a story by changing writers to include as many students as possible. At the end of such an activity, students are curious to read stories that they took part in and to find out how others developed their input. Dictations can also be very interactive; the usual pattern involves the teacher dictating to the students, but once they have the idea and an example, students can be challenged to design their own (Activities 44-45).

Writing from non-textual stimuli
Pictures and music are both media that can inspire written reactions, but of course they don't provide language input, so the students have to work from their own resources (Activities 47, 53 (variation 1) and 65). Brainstorming, and advice about style and structure, will go a long way towards helping the students produce a satisfactory text.

Writing freely
With most students, it is only after preparation, stimuli and inspiration (such as is outlined above) that they can get to the stage of writing freely. For the fortunate few, simply giving a title may be enough, but they would still benefit from preparing the ground beforehand. Word processors are invaluable aids to writing, as the student can chop and change the text at will, including after correction, and the finished product is always clearly legible and looks professional.

Conclusion

If we ask students to write whatever they please, we are in danger of setting a difficult and unrealistic task: we rarely write without a reason. Freedom can be restrictive and, without prompting or external stimuli, students can easily suffer 'writer's block'. In-class practice and a variety of progressive approaches can prepare them to feel inspiration and develop the skills to turn that inspiration into text.

Activity 54

When This Day is Done

Level	Intermediate onwards
Aims	Practising speaking; raising awareness of literary interpretation
Duration	15 minutes
Materials	Blank paper; the text
Preparation	None

Procedure

1. Dictate the following text:
   When this day is done time will fly into the trees and the clock will bang on the light of the cathedral.
2. Ask the students to discuss what the quotation means, in pairs or in groups.
3. Invite them to give feedback to the whole class.
4. Explain the origin of the text (see Note 1).

Variations

1. Any ambiguous text can lend itself to this activity.
2. If you are short on lesson time, you could write the quotation on the board or display it on the OHP, but dictating is truly MINIMAX!

Notes

1. This was said by a very tired 3-year-old boy. No poetic meaning was believed to have been intended.
2. You can suggest, if they believe it to be poetry, that *they* are the real poets, concluding perhaps that poetry may only exist if there are readers to appreciate it.
3. This activity works well as a lead-in to creative writing.

Activity 55

Draw the Poem

Level	Elementary onwards
Aims	Practising listening, writing and speaking
Duration	10-15 minutes
Materials	Paper; a poem
Preparation	None

Procedure

1. Make sure everyone has a pencil and some paper.
2. Read a poem aloud. Repeat it as many times as necessary (see Note 1).
3. As you read it, the students draw what they hear on their paper. You can suggest they use several colours in their drawings.
4. When you have finished, ask them to form pairs and explain to their partner what the things they have drawn represent.
5. They try to reconstruct the poem from the contents of their drawings.
6. Display the pictures, if you wish.

Variations

1. You could record the poem onto a cassette to save having to repeat it yourself in class, but this adds to preparation time.
2. A song can be used instead of a poem. Repeat the song at the end of the activity. This aids weaker listeners, who will recognise much more, having reconstructed it with a partner. The song I use is *What a Wonderful World* by Louis Armstrong. This then leads on to the themes of childhood, nature, world problems, etc.

Notes

1. The students can decide how many times you repeat the poem.
2. Not all poems lend themselves to drawing. If you are unsure, try drawing it yourself beforehand.
3. The paired discussion and text reconstruction are vital elements in this activity, as the students have to pay close attention to language detail.

Activity 56

Poem Shuffle

Level	Intermediate onwards
Aims	Practising reading; raising poetic awareness
Duration	20 minutes
Materials	A poem, cut into lines, for each group (see Note 1)
Preparation	10 minutes (the first time you do the activity only)

Procedure

1 Divide the class into groups of about four.

2 Give each group a copy of the poem, cut up and jumbled.

3 They put the poem into an order they find pleasing.

4 Ask a volunteer from each group to read out their version to the class.

Variations

1 They could write out their version onto a transparency for the OHP, but reading aloud saves time.

2 You can show them the original version if you wish.

Notes

1 Be careful here! Most poems do not lend themselves to cutting up, and it could be disrespectful. The type of poem it suits has only two rhyming sounds throughout, and the lines are complete sentences, such that changing the order does not affect the meaning conveyed or the style. An excellent poem for this activity is *Lonely Hearts* by Wendy Cope. It deals with the topic of personal columns in the press, relationships, etc.

2 Once you have cut up copies of the poem, keep them for future use.

3 Students must understand that they don't have to guess what the original poem was, they simply have to design their own poem from the lines given. Their version should not be seen as inferior to the original.

Activity 57

Ode to an Object

Level	Intermediate onwards
Aims	Practising writing and vocabulary; creating an unexpected poem
Duration	15-20 minutes
Materials	Blank paper
Preparation	None

Procedure

1 Ask students to write short answers, one below the other, to the following questions or prompts:

1 *Name an object you'd like to write about.*
2 *Write two adjectives to describe it.*
3 *Where is it?*
4 *Repeat its name.*
5 *What is it doing?*
6 *How is it doing it? (write adverbs)*
7 *Repeat where it is.*
8 *Repeat the two adjectives.*
9 *Add two more adjectives.*
10 *Repeat the name again.*

2 Help with the language where necessary.

3 Tell the students that they have written a poem, and invite them to read it to each other.

4 Display their poems if you wish.

Variations

1 The exact order of the questions does not matter.

2 You can include your own questions.

Notes

Here is an example:

The moon
Bright, silver
In the night sky
The moon
Spinning through space
Silently, slowly
In the night sky
Bright, silver
Shining, lost
The moon

Activity 58
Prompted Poem

Level	Intermediate onwards
Aims	Practising writing and vocabulary
Duration	15-20 minutes
Materials	Photocopies of the Poem Prompt
Preparation	2 minutes (to make the photocopies)

Procedure

1. Photocopy the Poem Prompt.
2. Give a list of themes and ask the students to choose one they would like to write about.
3. Give each student a copy of the Poem Prompt.
4. Ask them to fill in the gaps as they wish.
5. Invite volunteers to read their poems to the class.
6. Display the poems if you wish.

Variations

1. A list of topics might include the following: love, happiness, truth, fear, courage, loneliness, jealousy, greed, violence, peace, war, light, darkness, pain, joy, money, friendship, poetry, art, music, etc.
2. You could allocate topics yourself if the students are reluctant to choose.
3. They could pick their topic at random.

Notes

In the Poem Prompt, *___________* is the theme, and the students write their own words where there are spaces (..................).

DESIGNED TO PHOTOCOPY

Poem Prompt

____

_____________ is the colour of ....

....

I feel it when I ....

It sounds like ....

and many people think it is ....

....

When we live with *_____________*

we ....

....

It tastes of .... and

....

and I see it in my ....

I dream of *_____________* when I

....

....

And I hope that one day *_____________*

....

....

Activity 59

Love Is ...

Level	Intermediate onwards (This activity works well for teachers, too.)
Aims	Practising writing
Duration	15 minutes
Materials	Blank paper
Preparation	None

Procedure

1. Choose a topic, such as love.
2. Ask each student to write one sentence, starting *Love is ...* .
3. Divide the class into groups of eight to ten students.
4. They arrange their sentences in a sequence that is pleasing to them.
5. Ask a volunteer from each group to read out the result to the whole class.

Variations

1. Topics might include the following: happiness, honesty, war, music, friendship, home. A successful version for teachers starts with *Teaching is ...* .
2. You can ask the students to write out their texts onto a transparency for the OHP. (This takes longer.)

Notes

The encouraging result of this activity is that a poem is created from sentences which were not intended to be poetic.

Activity 60

Theme Alphabets

Level	Intermediate onwards
Aims	Practising relative clauses, cause and effect clauses, sentence construction and vocabulary
Duration	20-30 minutes
Materials	Blank paper
Preparation	None

Procedure

1. Revise the alphabet with the class and choose a theme, eg. love.
2. Explain that the idea is to write a sentence, for every letter of the alphabet, following the format:
   A is for ..., because ...
   or
   A is for ..., which ...
3. Divide the class into groups.
4. When everyone has finished, listen to the contributions from each group.
5. Collect and display the entries if you wish.

Variation

If you are short on time, each group can take just a section of the alphabet.

Notes

1. It will help to give an example, eg:
   A is for address book, where you keep your lovers' phone numbers.
   A is for amorous, which is how you feel when you're drunk.
2. Challenge the students to write better ones.
3. A great deal of humour can come out of this activity, eg:
   U is for unhappy, which is how people look when they're in love.

Activity 61
Mini-sagas

Level	Intermediate onwards
Aims	Practising writing
Duration	30-40 minutes
Materials	Blank paper
Preparation	None

Procedure

1. Explain to the class that they are about to write a very short story. Give some time for thinking about it.
2. Tell the students that there are certain constraints:
   - The story must be exactly 50 words long.
   - It must have a beginning, a development and an ending.
   - It must have characters and a setting.
   - The title may contain up to 15 additional words.
3. Allow at least 20 minutes for writing.
4. Invite the students to read out their mini-sagas.

Variations

1. You may prefer to set a topic or a limited choice of topics.
2. Time and other constraints can be varied as you wish.

Notes

1. It is advisable for students to write the story first, then cut it down afterwards.
2. Insisting on economy of language forces students to consider what is linguistically important, and what is superfluous, for conveying an idea.
3. Economy can also result in poetic and philosophical styles which were unintentional.

Here is an example of a mini-saga:
The Postcard
Friendless, he despatched a letter to the twelfth century. Illuminated scrolls arrived by return post. Jottings to Tutankhamun secured hieroglyphs on papyrus; Hannibal sent a campaign report. But when he addressed the future, hoping for cassettes crammed with wonders, a postcard drifted back with scorched edges. It glowed all night.
(from Ron White and Valerie Arndt. 1991. *Process Writing*. Harlow: Longman.)

Activity 62
Construct-Deconstruct

Level	Intermediate onwards
Aims	Practising sentence construction
Duration	20 minutes
Materials	None
Preparation	None

Procedure

1. Brainstorm with the class a theme, eg. a place, a person, or an abstract topic such as 'language'.
2. Challenge the class individually, in pairs or in groups, to write one sentence which incorporates as many ideas from the brainstorm session as possible. The sentence must be grammatically correct and must make perfect sense.
3. Choose one of the sentences and ask the creator to write it on the board.
4. Now ask the students to look at the long sentence on the board, and in turn, remove a section of up to three consecutive words from the sentence. The sentence must still be grammatically correct and make perfect sense, although the meaning may change.
5. Stop when you are down to a few words, or there is just one word left on the board.
6. Now ask the students to form groups, taking it in turns to add up to three words at a time to the words that were left on the board.
7. They write each new sentence afresh on a piece of paper. Again, each new sentence must be grammatically correct and make perfect sense.
8. The aim is to try and reconstruct the original sentence which was on the board.

Variations

1. The initial brainstorm can be in groups.
2. You may like to do the reconstruction as a whole-class activity.
3. You can allow the students to reconstruct any sentence they like, while following the constraints of the activity.

(continued on next page)

Notes

1. The advantage of reconstructing the same sentence is one of activating the memory and encouraging weaker students, who have seen the target sentence already on the board. They may find it easier to remember that, than have to create a new sentence.

2. The students will monitor the language themselves, rejecting ungrammatical or unfeasible language. However, make sure you are also monitoring.

Activity 63

Dear Object

Level	Intermediate onwards
Aims	Practising letter writing and speaking
Duration	30 minutes
Materials	Blank paper
Preparation	None

Procedure

1. Ask the class to think of an object they would like to be, eg. a gadget, a toy, a musical instrument, etc.

2. In pairs, encourage each student to talk to their partner 'in role', answering questions about being that particular object.

3. Arrange the students in circles of eight to ten, still keeping the same pairs.

4. Each person introduces their partner as the object they have chosen to be.

5. Everyone now writes a letter to any 'object' that was introduced to them, asking any questions they like.

6. The 'objects' who receive letters write back to the students who wrote to them.

7. Students and objects continue to exchange notes for as long as interest lasts (half an hour should be plenty of time).

Variations

1. You can also have 'objects' writing to other 'objects'.

2. The students can choose a famous person as a role instead of an object, and they can write to each other in role.

3. The students can write to each other as themselves, without adopting any role.

Notes

Make sure everyone is engaged. Some students might receive more mail than others, but as long as they all write, they should all get an answer eventually. The more letters they write, the more answers they should receive. You can also participate yourself, so as to activate the students who are idly waiting for replies.

Activity 64
Genre Circle Writing

Level	Advanced
Aims	Practising narration; exploring sensitivity to genre
Duration	30 minutes
Materials	Blank paper
Preparation	None

Procedure

1. Brainstorm types of narrative genres, eg. news article, whodunnit, romance, sci-fi, western, comedy, nursery rhyme, conversation, kidnap note, speech, fairy tale, formal/informal letter, Tarantinoesque, Shakespearean, etc.
2. Ask each student to choose the genre they would like to write in.
3. Encourage them to think what makes their genre recognisable, eg. vocabulary, fixed expressions, sequence, word and sentence length, register, readership, bias, etc.
4. Arrange them in circles of six, each student with a different genre.
5. Each student thinks of the start of a story and writes it at the top of a sheet of paper (just one paragraph), giving it a title.
6. After an agreed time limit, eg. five minutes, they pass their papers to the left.
7. The students read the new story and continue it, changing the genre to their own.
8. This continues until the story gets back to its originator.

Variation

You can vary the number of genres and the circle size to match.

Notes

Allow all the students to read or hear all the stories, eg. by displaying them. There is a good reason to listen or read, as they have all contributed and will be curious to see what happened next.

Activity 65
Musical Circle Writing

Level	Intermediate onwards
Aims	Practising narration; exploiting musical sensitivity
Duration	30 minutes
Materials	Cassette of six to eight short extracts (3 minutes each) of varied music; blank paper
Preparation	None (if you have the cassette ready)

Procedure

1. Arrange the students in circles of six to eight.
2. Explain that when the music starts, everyone will start writing a story. One or two sentences is enough.
3. When the music changes, they pass the story to the left.
4. Each student reads the new story and continues it until the music changes. Students should let their writing be inspired and guided by the different types of music.
5. The story is passed on and continued every time the music changes.
6. Finally, the story reaches the student who started it, who reads it.

Variations

1. You can vary the number of pieces of music and the circle size to match.
2. You might like to play the music through first (or, more realistically, in shorter extracts of 30 seconds) to sensitise the students. They can be encouraged to say or write how they feel in response to the music, or think about adjectives which describe the music.

Notes

1. You can brainstorm themes for stories beforehand, and match these up with the (shortened) musical pieces.
2. Allow all the students to read or hear all the stories, eg. by displaying them. There is a good reason to listen or read, as they have all contributed and will be curious to see what happened next.

Chapter **6**

Dealing with Diversity

Learners are unique while being at the same time members of a group. For effective teaching and learning to take place, we need to accommodate this dichotomy in the classroom. Individual sensitivities and group dynamics have to be balanced.

Diverse learning sensitivities

Your activities and techniques will only motivate some of your students at any given time. It may be most of them, it will probably not be all of them. This is only to be expected. And if you only concentrate on a limited number of approaches, then you may be ignoring opportunities to engage more of your students. You will have noticed how students' responses to activities can vary. One reason is that we are all sensitive to different stimuli in different degrees: we learn, and like to learn, in different ways.

Here are the most common sensitivities, but it is important to note that they overlap, and to remember that most people respond to a mixture of stimuli:

Sensitivities	Respond to
VISUAL	reading, writing, looking, watching; pictures, colour, diagrams, moving images
AUDITORY	listening, speaking; music, film
KINESTHETIC	touching, moving, creating; sports, active games
OLFATORY	aromas and smells
GUSTATORY	the sense of taste
LOGICAL-MATHEMATICAL	puzzling out; numbers, rules, logic
MUSICAL	singing, dancing, listening; rhythms
SPATIAL	drawing, designing, arranging, sculpting, mapping, moving, orienteering
LINGUISTIC	reading and writing; wordgames, language structure
NATURALISTIC	looking after living things, cultivating plants, studying ecosystems; the natural world
INTUITIVE	intuition, guesswork, prediction
INTERPERSONAL	working together, communicating, meeting, socialising, speaking
INTRAPERSONAL	reflecting, working individually

(See Gardner, Grinder, Revell and Norman, and Wingate in the Bibliography.)

It is easy to understand why not all of your students will share your enthusiasm for songs, for example. As you play a song, remember that some students will read or listen quietly, others will focus better with a task to do, some will write, others tap their feet, others will look out of the window, some may enjoy dancing or singing, while others may be concentrating on the sound of the electric guitar. By the law of averages it is only fair to expect that a few will be unimpressed or even bored, and one or two may hate the sound! Some will appreciate the poetry of the lyrics while others will miss the message completely. This will happen whatever the song or whoever chooses it: there is no perfect song for class use, just as there is no perfect lesson. The saving grace must lie in variety, so next time you play a song, choose a completely different style of music.

Diverse learning styles

As well as being differentially sensitive and motivated, students also learn and participate in class in different ways. There are several classifications, and it is interesting to reflect on how successful learning and successful teaching may be dependent on an awareness of student preferences.

Here is one classification:

Learner	Likes
ACCOMMODATOR	getting involved, taking risks, adapting to trial and error, learning by doing, using intuition
ASSIMILATOR	thinking and reasoning, planning and applying theory, logic
CONVERGER	practical applications, decision making, working individually, looking for one best answer
DIVERGER	involving the imagination and emotions, working with others, accepting a broad range of ideas or possible answers

(See Kolb in the Bibliography.)

Rightly or wrongly, we may worry if a student doesn't join in with the others or is reluctant to work in pairs. There may be social tensions in the group that we need to monitor, or it may just be that the student is primarily an independent 'converger', with strong intrapersonal sensitivities. Perhaps we should think twice about forcing students to form groups.

Here is a second classification:

Learners	Features
ACTIVISTS	people who are happy to participate openly and readily in new experiences, taking central roles and looking for excitement
REFLECTORS	cautious, thoughtful people who like observing, listening and considering thoroughly before acting, reaching conclusions or making decisions
THEORISTS	logical, objective people who like analysing, making rules and theories
PRAGMATISTS	practical people who like putting theories into practice, making decisions and solving problems

(See Honey and Mumford in the Bibliography.)

We do our students a disservice if we treat them as if they were all alike. They may all have to learn to give presentations, for example, but it might be unfair to nominate a 'reflector' to go first, when an 'activist' is begging for an opportunity to 'have a go'. Both can learn from the triumphs and mistakes of the latter. It is not just vacillation on the part of the teacher to ask if anyone would like to go first.

Most learners are probably mixtures of these styles, and one particular learner may change according to mood or motivation. A danger of identifying learner types is that students might label themselves and, at the extreme, use that classification as an excuse not to participate fully and openly in certain learning experiences. They need to know the relative advantages and disadvantages of each learning style: for instance, the issue of self-consciousness in the face of error.

Investigating diversity

Finding out about learner differences can be fun, and may constitute a lesson in itself. This is useful information which can guide you, not only in planning your syllabus but also in identifying learning problems. In a sense, therefore, it is a type of Needs Analysis. Questionnaires can serve this purpose very successfully.

Look at the *Learner Sensitivities Questionnaire* on page 79. There are no correct answers, and students can tick as many items as they like. The names of the sensitivities are withheld until afterwards, to avoid self-labelling. The discussion that follows can lead into school experiences, the curriculum, coursebook evaluation, exams and systems of assessment.

Key to Learner Sensitivities Questionnaire:

Logical-Mathematical	2
Musical	4
Visual-Spatial	3
Bodily-Kinesthetic	5
Interpersonal	6
Linguistic	1
Intrapersonal	7

Dealing with diversity

Language teachers need not despair at those students who don't exhibit predictable linguistic tendencies. Progress may lie in the adoption of a multiple-sensitory approach.

Consider the numerous ways of learning vocabulary:

LINGUISTICALLY	translating, categorising words according to stress patterns, learning rhymes, playing games with wordcards, studying vocabulary on the computer (eg. concordancing), using dictionaries and lexicons, learning lists by heart
SPATIALLY	grouping words into families, mind-mapping, making posters and wall displays
VISUALLY	highlighting in colour, drawing diagrams, using small rods (Cuisenaire rods) of different lengths and colours (Activity 74)
KINESTHETICALLY	rods, drama, activities like 'stand up when you hear a particular word in a story', clicking a computer mouse
AUDITORILY	cassettes and films
MUSICALLY	singing songs, rhythmic chants, nursery rhymes
INTUITIVELY	guessing the meaning of unfamiliar words, matching exercises

We need to expose learners to the choices available, because just being sensitive to certain channels is not enough. Students may not know about or have access to computers, rods, videos, drama experiences and other techniques. Talking about the different ways of recording vocabulary (part of fostering study skills) will form a useful part of a lesson early in the course.

Varying the channel of sensitivity or response may stimulate motivation for learning in learners experiencing difficulty. We have looked at vocabulary, now let us consider grammar, for example the language of speculation involving modal verbs (*must, could, may, might, couldn't, can't*).

This may be presented (or revised) in many ways, including the following:

VISUALLY	Draw something on the board in stages; at each stage elicit suggestions of what it might be (*It must be something round, It might be a clock, It can't be a pyramid,* etc.). Ambiguous photos are useful for this, too.
AUDITORILY	Play a cassette of strange sounds, a quiz of filmstars' voices, or ask students to guess the intonation (*He may be angry,* etc.).
MUSICALLY	Prepare a quiz of well-known pop-singers and composers.
KINESTHETICALLY	Ask students to mime actions, locations, occupations, etc. (*She could be playing cards, in a bank, an accountant,* etc.). Realia may help: strange objects can inspire guessing for purpose, or a bag with contents can be used to make deductions about the owner (*She must like reading because she's carrying a book*).
OLFATO-GUSTATORILY	Invite students to guess foodstuffs blindfold, or try to tell Pepsi from Coke (*This can't be Coke because it's too sweet*).
SPATIALLY	Describe your own house, city, country, and ask the students to draw a map in pairs. Then present the map to the class (*We think the swimming pool may be here as it's next to the sports centre*).
LOGICALLY	Give logic puzzles to solve (Activity 83), perform magic tricks, present murder mysteries.
LINGUISTICALLY	Play with word games, anagrams, matching words to definitions, crosswords.

Emotion and learning

Another factor which makes learning memorable is having fun, which of course may mean different things to different people, so again variety is the key. The brain's limbic system enhances the learning process by connecting what is to be learnt with the learner's emotions and state of mind. In short, you learn better if it's funny, or scary, or curious, or surprising; or, in the case of music or art, simply pleasurable. But how, and to what extent, can emotion become part of a lesson?

A classroom atmosphere which is relaxed enough to include humour will create a positive experience and enhance the desire to attend, with positive implications for study and even homework (Activities 78 and 80). But jokes can also be a central part of the lesson (Activity 82). Storytelling naturally includes joke-telling, and many jokes reflect linguistic play and cultural patterns. A great deal of authentic literature in English uses wordplay, from advertisements to headlines in magazines. This must be a challenge to even the most proficient students. Sensitising students to language play, therefore, not only provides motivation through amusement but also opens a window onto culture.

Other emotions can be exploited for memorable learning. Tension through competition, curiosity about the bizarre, and surprise at mysteries and tricks can all add enjoyment to lessons (Activity 83). Even fear can play a part, if you black out the windows and tell horror stories by candlelight. Music plays on many emotions (Activity 65), and it is recommendable to keep a stock of songs and activities that seem to work again and again. (Activities 84-85 are standards which are always appreciated.)

Heterogeneous classes

You can almost certainly guarantee that all your students are learning, but some will learn more quickly than others. Also, they will have started off unequally: some will have scored higher than others in the entrance exam, their educational backgrounds may differ, and there will be differences in attitude to education, which may be reflected in behaviour, participation and body language. In addition, some students like to be in a challenging level while others prefer being in a class where they feel more comfortable.

We as teachers have to acknowledge that students vary in 'strength', but we should not look upon this strength as carved in stone, and should avoid labelling and self-fulfilling prophecies. We should envisage strength as a developing, dynamic thing, and accept our role as one which is instrumental in bringing about such change. The important thing is to be aware of students' differences and see the situation as one in flux, constantly changing. Be open to the likelihood that a particular learner may be a slow reader but a perceptive listener, or that by reading slowly they may acquire more language than someone who reads fast. Remember, too, that a slow reader may love reading. Many of these relative 'weaknesses' can be improved in time and with practice, under your guidance and watchful eye.

Problems of heterogeneity

A major problem is that it is difficult to gauge the level at which you should pitch the lesson, and there are differences in what is comprehensible input. Some students understand if you speak normally while others require more graded language. The former will speak in such a way that the latter might not understand, and tend to jump in with contributions without allowing others to reflect.

Some students finish tasks well before others, and get bored when having to listen to presentations or explanations which are already familiar and clear, or they get impatient working with their slower peers. Other students feel intimidated and refuse to participate, even blocking their own learning, sometimes seeking attention in negative, disruptive ways. In this way they miss more input and practice and appear to fall further behind; indeed if recycling doesn't take place as it should then retention will be impaired.

It is difficult to know whether to group stronger and weaker students together or to keep them apart, not just for pedagogic reasons, as students may resist certain grouping combinations. Also it is difficult to know whether to treat all students as if they were alike, or to recognise that there are differences, and acknowledge them to the students.

Dealing with heterogeneity

While there are no universal remedies or easy answers, there are a number of strategies that might be attempted in order to solve some of these problems. You will recognise some of them from earlier chapters.

Getting to know your students

Try to collect as much information as you can about your students by asking them to discuss and fill in questionnaires in class and at home. If you do a Needs Analysis or a Learner Style and Preference survey, you can then act on it to design a suitable course and distribute certain learning tasks.

If a student likes reading in English or would like to read more, find out what kind of reading they like and make sure they obtain access to it. Not only will they enjoy the reading material, but they will appreciate your efforts.

If students acknowledge that they don't enjoy English or English classes, try to find out why, and attempt to act on that information. In some schools, it may be convenient to talk to the students' previous teachers to get more background information, but be careful to filter the information so that your judgement is free of prejudice.

Self-evaluation, continuous assessment and counselling

Information-seeking should continue through the course. You need to know how things are going for the students. And they need to see that you are interested, and have the chance to reflect on their learning. They need information, too, about their progress, strengths, weaknesses and attitude from your perception. It is unsatisfactory and frustrating to fail a course as a surprise. If failure looks likely early on, steps can and should be taken there and then. This information exchange can be done in writing by means of forms, mid-term reports, questionnaires, and so on, but oral feedback can be given through individual counselling.

Counselling can be done in class time by organising tasks for the whole group to do while you interview each student one-by-one outside, not too far away. In the case of young learners, parents' meetings are extremely useful and informative for both parent and teacher, but the student would also benefit from and appreciate consultation, especially if there is praise where it is due.

However, counselling needs preparation. The students need time to reflect and prepare their comments, so a self-evaluation form can be given out for homework beforehand. This will encourage the learners to think about and assess their own strengths and weaknesses, and consider what they need to do to improve. In a two-minute interview it is possible to find out if the students are happy and can see progress or if they are bored, floundering or unchallenged. Furthermore, telling you may be a weight off their minds!

Classroom control and organisation

The best approach to diversity is variety, and lessons should be varied enough to cater for reasonable attention spans, with the need for rest periods and diversions, such as energisers. It may sound unrealistically simple but is always useful to keep in mind that busy students don't have time to waste on negative distractions. Teachers may sometimes feel they are losing control. This is because they try and control everything, to the frustration, perhaps, of some students. Handing over control in some classroom events gives them responsibility, enhancing their conscientiousness and avoiding distraction.

Involving students in their own learning

Stronger students can offer input through elicitation while weaker students listen and absorb it. Teacher reinforcement adds exposure and confirmation. Students already familiar with a structure may take more responsibility for presenting and explaining, thus preventing them getting bored, giving other students exposure (which you may reinforce) and minimising your own input.

If the activity is meaning-focused, it may engage students who already know the language forms being practised, so personalised and open-ended activities (see Chapter 2) may help. If they design their own activities (see Chapter 3), faster finishers can be given extra work such as extending tasks or designing new ones. Also, as they work in groups, students will brainstorm together and share new language. Furthermore, as students correct each other's performance, it is possible to find weaker students correcting and giving feedback on stronger students' work.

Developing study skills

A useful part of a teacher's role is to teach students to help themselves, thus increasing learning potential while saving the teacher unnecessary effort. One element is to teach how resources such as reference books (including dictionaries and the coursebook), the phonemic chart, computers and self-access centres can be exploited. This can be done by demonstration, guided discovery, quizzes and competitions, and by setting tasks for students to complete.

Another strategy is to train students to keep good notes, allowing choice for individual learning preferences. They can store vocabulary in different ways: in random lists, with accompanying translations, in pictorial form, in sentence context, or grouped in families or lexical sets (these are diverse in themselves: synonyms, antonyms, graded opposites, homonyms, homographs, homophones, or merely according to theme).

Subskills of the Four Skills can be fostered because, once acquired, they serve the learner independently thereafter. Receptive skills - intensive and extensive, as well as dealing with unknown vocabulary - can be practised in class, so that the students can read and listen at home in their own time.

Promoting autonomy through self-access

Some schools have a self-access centre in which students can study independently at their own speed. Students still need guidance in this before they can be truly independent (see *Developing study skills* above). They need to know what resources are available, how to use and look after them, and how best to learn from them.

But it doesn't have to be a separate centre. You could have a self-access box or envelope in the classroom. This would contain extra tasks for fast finishers, such as the slips of paper from *Word Pancakes* (Activity 39) or the cards from *Loop Card Transformations* (Activity 48), photos, grammar exercises, reading texts, past papers of exams, and so on. As well as reading a text from the self-access box, a student may design a comprehension task to go with it, or complete a task that someone else has put in. Pairs of students can test each other on vocabulary (on paper slips) while they are waiting for others to finish a task.

Providing extra tasks can often be a burden for teachers, unless the students create them themselves, or unless the coursebook is rich in practice material. If everybody does the same task at the same time, and everyone has to finish or stop before going on to the next stage, learner diversity generates periods of dead time and frustration. Extra tasks may help, but if students are working more independently on tasks which differ in length, complexity and number, then there is less wasted time and more challenge. Furthermore, differences in student performance and pace are less conspicuous.

Project work

Project work is a natural and logical extension of autonomous, self-directed learning. A project is an extended piece of work over time, with a 'product' in view: a presentation, or materials such as posters, magazines, radio or TV programmes, and so on. Projects can be done individually, in pairs, in groups, or as a whole-class activity. Plenty of guidance is needed to get started, especially if the idea is new, but after that much of the research, decision-making, creation, presentation and learning can be left in the students' hands.

Simulations

A simulation is a task like a role-play, except that the students play themselves. It is a mini-project, which may only last one session, such as designing a radio programme or planning a summer school course. Each student may have a job to do, such as editor, DJ, sound technician, etc., but they don't have to go into role in order to perform it. Although the task and the time limit may be set by the teacher, the students are responsible for getting the work done in their own way. Doing this in teams adds competition and also provides an audience for the finished product.

Presentations

Students can be encouraged to give presentations to small groups or to the whole class. This can be challenging and exciting, and stronger students still face a challenge of nerves even if they are relaxed about the language. Nobody should be forced, however, and apprehension should be treated in a serious, sympathetic light rather than ridiculed. Weaker students will also benefit enormously from giving a talk, and you can offer more help with language, style and content 'behind the scenes', even running through a rehearsal if this seems a good idea.

Five minutes is long enough for a presentation, and students should practise timing it beforehand. You can suggest a list of topics, based on the syllabus (or typical exam question topics), for them to choose from, or they can choose their own topic. It is advisable to give the listeners a reason to listen. This may be a task (why not allow it to be set by the speaker?), the result of an intriguing introduction, or the insistence of a question from everyone at the end.

Graded tasks

A strategy to deal with diverse working speeds is to have groups working on different tasks, or the same task at different levels.

If an exercise in the coursebook has ten questions, some groups can be given fewer questions to answer, to allow them more time for reading and thinking. They can choose their own questions. This means that they will read more than is required in order to make their choice. Those looking for a challenge can attempt the more difficult ones, and you have more material for fast finishers.

In a dictation students can be given different tasks according to level: a strong group writes down everything, another fills gaps while a weaker group fills gaps from a choice of answers. This technique has the advantage that when the students are re-grouped to check the answers together, the weaker ones can help the stronger ones to correct their texts, as they will be in possession of the complete passage, perfectly spelt.

It may be quite difficult in practice to sort the class into streamed groups without making it obvious. One solution is to allow them to choose which group they'd like to join or which activity they would prefer to do. Or you might arrange the groups before the class, associate each group with a colour and give each student a coloured card, telling them to work with those who have the same colour. For the sake of variety, try to avoid having the same groups every lesson.

Groups of students can be given different questions, varying in level, to accompany a reading text, or they can ask their own comprehension questions. After this the questions are handed in, and then there can be a quiz stage after the groups have been reshuffled. During this type of collaborative quiz, weaker students who have pre-viewed or designed a particular question could help stronger students who have not. (Activity 41 includes such a quiz and Activity 87 proposes another collaborative task.)

Adapted tasks

Almost any task can be modified to make it easier or more difficult. A common exercise in tests and coursebooks is a 'gapfill' text (a passage of text with gaps to fill in).

To increase the level of difficulty you can:

- increase the number or frequency of the gaps.
- mix the order of paragraphs.
- remove titles and subheadings.
- limit the time available for the task.
- withhold important background information.
- withhold advice about how to tackle the exercise.
- choose a longer or more difficult text.

To decrease the level of difficulty you can:

- decrease the number or frequency of the gaps.
- give verb stems (in the case of tense manipulation exercises).
- supply the first letter of each missing word.
- offer a choice of words to choose from.
- give the answers in anagram form.
- indicate which part of speech each answer is (noun, verb, adjective, etc.).
- allow more time for the task.
- provide background information about the text.
- give a summary of the content of the text.
- offer advice about how to tackle the task.
- choose a shorter or easier text.

Pre-task tasks
All students tend to benefit from extra exposure to texts, so a useful technique is to ask students to read a text, design tasks (such as comprehension questions), then keep those tasks for a later lesson. This works particularly well with listening activities. (Activity 43)

The tapescript can be used as a reading text first of all, and students can explore the language and meaning as they prepare their own comprehension questions. Some time later the text may be used for listening practice, and the students' questions could be used, swapping them over so that each group answers another group's questions. Weaker students might do pre-task work on a listening text which no-one else sees, so that when it comes to the listening activity, they have an advantage over other students without anybody realising.

Teaching to different sensitivities

At the very beginning of this book, we insisted on the need for balance. Throughout a course, and when presenting language or devising activities, it is fundamental to bear in mind the channel and sensitivity (visual, etc.), in order to cater to different types of learners at different times, and to strive to provide a balance over a given period of time. Variety may be less essential where motivation is already extremely high, but most students would probably agree that variety is far more motivating than monotony. Activities 66-87 provide examples of classroom activities designed to appeal to a range of sensitivities.

Let us finish by suggesting four strategic areas for dealing with the effects of diversity and heterogeneity:

Differentiate:
- the amount of help you give each group.
- the level, length and number of tasks.
- the time allowed for a task, including rehearsal time.

Vary:
- the sensitivity focus.
- the type of lesson (skills work, grammar focus, vocabulary practice).
- the pace and activity in a lesson.
- the focus (who is talking).
- the materials and equipment used.
- the teacher-centred/learner-centred balance.

Equalise:
- the attention you give each student in class.
- the care and consultation you give.
- student talking time.

Promote:
- study skills.
- self-access.
- independence and autonomy.

Conclusion

When we talk about whether or not a class is learning, we really need to examine the progress of each individual. A class of 30 students is a group of 30 individuals, not a 30-fold learning army. A regimented, uniform syllabus is therefore inappropriate for maximising the learning potential of the class. What is more appropriate is an approach that combines equalisation and differentiation, autonomy and variety. This does not mean that teachers must exhaust themselves in the attempt to provide it. What this chapter, and indeed the whole book, has tried to demonstrate, is that the students themselves can be instruments in achieving their own optimal learning environment, under the watchful eye of the MINIMAX teacher.

Learner Sensitivities Questionnaire

Tick if the statement is true for you.

Sensitivity Number 1

- ☐ I can imagine how a word sounds.
- ☐ I learn more from the radio than from the TV.
- ☐ I like wordgames.
- ☐ I enjoy tongue twisters.
- ☐ I like wordplay and puns.
- ☐ I have a good vocabulary.
- ☐ I prefer arts to sciences.
- ☐ I like reading.
- ☐ I enjoy writing.
- ☐ I speak a foreign language.

Sensitivity Number 2

- ☐ I can work out calculations in my head.
- ☐ I play chess or other strategy games.
- ☐ I'm curious about how things work.
- ☐ I think most things have a logical explanation.
- ☐ I'm more logical than a lot of people I know.
- ☐ I like things to be measurable or quantifiable.
- ☐ I enjoy detective mysteries.
- ☐ I like logic puzzles.
- ☐ I can see the consequences of actions easily.
- ☐ I prefer sciences to arts.

Sensitivity Number 3

- ☐ I can see clear images when I close my eyes.
- ☐ I like using a camera.
- ☐ I enjoy visual puzzles such as jigsaws.
- ☐ I have vivid dreams at night.
- ☐ I find maps interesting.
- ☐ I have a good sense of direction.
- ☐ I prefer geometry to algebra.
- ☐ I appreciate tasteful decoration and dress sense.
- ☐ I like drawing and painting.
- ☐ I enjoy looking at art in books or galleries.

Sensitivity Number 4

- ☐ I enjoy listening to music.
- ☐ I can follow a rhythm.
- ☐ I often sing, hum or whistle to myself.
- ☐ I'm good at recognising tunes.
- ☐ I can sing quite well.
- ☐ I can tell if a note is off-key.
- ☐ I play a musical instrument.
- ☐ I enjoy dancing.
- ☐ I can remember tunes well.
- ☐ I often tap out rhythms when concentrating.

Sensitivity Number 5

- ☐ I play sport regularly.
- ☐ I get restless sitting still.
- ☐ I fidget or draw doodles when concentrating.
- ☐ I like working with my hands and physical work.
- ☐ I like sculpture.
- ☐ I enjoy dancing.
- ☐ I make hand gestures when I speak.
- ☐ I learn by doing.
- ☐ I like funfair rides.
- ☐ Physical activity helps me think.

Sensitivity Number 6

- ☐ People come to me for advice.
- ☐ I prefer group sports to individual sports.
- ☐ I like to discuss a problem with someone.
- ☐ I like parties and social gatherings.
- ☐ I enjoy group games like playing cards.
- ☐ I like teaching people things.
- ☐ I'm quite a good leader.
- ☐ I like organising events.
- ☐ I feel comfortable in a crowd.
- ☐ I'd rather go out than stay in.

Sensitivity Number 7

- ☐ I like meditation.
- ☐ I often think about important things in life.
- ☐ I'm interested in self-improvement.
- ☐ People sometimes don't understand me.
- ☐ I'm quite independent.
- ☐ I enjoy being alone.
- ☐ I have hobbies I do alone or I keep secret.
- ☐ I have important goals for myself.
- ☐ I tend to remain quiet in a group.
- ☐ I keep a diary.

Match these names to Sensitivities 1-7:

Logical-Mathematical ......

Musical ......

Visual-Spatial ......

Bodily-Kinesthetic ......

Interpersonal ......

Linguistic ......

Intrapersonal ......

This questionnaire is adapted from the work of Jim Wingate. The key is on page 73.

Activity 66
Wearing Statues

Level	Elementary onwards
Aims	Energiser; practising the present continuous; clothes vocabulary
Duration	10 minutes
Materials	None
Preparation	None

Procedure

1. Brainstorm clothes vocabulary if necessary.
2. Ask the students to stand up and move around the room.
3. When you give a signal, they stand back-to-back with a partner.
4. Select one student to tell you what the other student is wearing (from memory, as they won't be able to see them).
5. Continue by asking other students.

Variations

1. You can play music, and when it stops the students find a partner.
2. Vary the question, eg. '*What colour shoes is she wearing?*'
3. In their pairs, the students can tell each other what they are wearing or ask each other questions, eg. '*Are you wearing ...?*'

Notes

1. Insist on full sentences, with the natural contraction, eg. *He's wearing ...* .
2. If you have an odd number of students, ask the one without a partner to take on your role as questioner, once you have demonstrated it.

Activity 67
You Have Changed

Level	Elementary onwards
Aims	Practising the present perfect; clothes vocabulary
Duration	10 minutes
Materials	None
Preparation	None

Procedure

1. Divide the class into groups of four to six students.
2. Ask each group to study the other groups.
3. Ask them all to turn away and make some changes to their appearance, eg. exchanging pullovers, changing a watch from one wrist to the other, removing rings, etc.
4. They present themselves to the other groups.
5. The other groups have to point out as many changes as they can see.

Variation

This can be done in pairs, sitting down, if necessary.

Notes

1. Try and insist on full sentences and plenty of practice for all.
2. Allow all correct, natural contributions, even if it isn't the present perfect, eg. *You're wearing a different bracelet.*

Activity 68

What am I Doing?

Level	Elementary onwards
Aims	Energiser; practising the present continuous
Duration	10 minutes
Materials	None
Preparation	None

Procedure

1. Ask the class to stand up in pairs.
2. Demonstrate with one student first. Ask them to ask you '*What am I doing?*'.
3. Give an imaginary answer, eg. '*You're fishing*'.
4. Explain or use gestures so that the student starts to mime 'fishing'.
5. Whilst they are fishing, ask them '*What am I doing?*' and they must give you an action to mime. While they think of an action, they mustn't stop fishing.
6. Suppose they say '*You're cleaning your teeth*', you now start miming cleaning your teeth, but must also encourage your partner to ask '*What am I doing?*' again, and you give them some other action to mime.
7. Once the rest of the class understand what to do, they can all work in pairs.

Variations

1. The same activity can be done in a circle.
2. An interesting variation is to ask '*What are you doing?*' and the student thinks of an action quite unrelated to the one they are miming. This is the cue for the first student to start miming this new action, during which they are asked '*What are you doing?*', and must think up something unrelated to their mime for their partner to do. The mismatch between what they are doing and what they say they are doing causes a good deal of amusement.

Notes

With all mime and drama activities, it is important that you not only join in, but are one of the first people to do so. If *you* are reluctant about it, you can't expect your students to take part whole-heartedly.

Activity 69

Earthquake!

Level	Elementary onwards
Aims	Energiser; practising relative and participle clauses and *if* sentences
Duration	10 minutes
Materials	None
Preparation	None

Procedure

1. Arrange the students in a circle, sitting on chairs. Two circles may be necessary in large classes.
2. Stand in the centre, without a chair.
3. Say '*Everyone who's wearing blue jeans, change places*'.
4. Everyone wearing blue jeans must stand up and sit in a new seat.
5. Repeat the activity with a different structure, eg. *All those who play basketball change places.*
6. Repeat the activity with a different structure, eg. *Change places if you've got a dog at home.*
7. When you have demonstrated enough, jump into a chair, leaving one of the students in the middle.
8. This student now has to get into a chair by continuing the process of getting the other students up and out of theirs.
9. Introduce a signal occasionally, at which everybody has to get up and change seats, eg. by shouting out '*Earthquake!*'.

Notes

Repeating the examples with different sentence structures shows the students that the structure and topic can vary, so there is more scope for their imaginations and for language practice.

Activity 70

Bombarding Questions

Level	Elementary onwards
Aims	Practising question formation; promoting fluency
Duration	10 minutes
Materials	None
Preparation	None

Procedure

1. Demonstrate first yourself. Ask students to ask you lots of questions about anything they like, for two minutes. Don't answer.

2. After two minutes, answer the questions you remember, or would like to answer.

3. Divide the class into groups of three or four, in which the students take it in turns to be bombarded.

Variations

1. You can give the students a particular topic to talk about, if you wish.

2. They can do this activity 'in role', too. Both those asking and those answering can assume a role, eg. it could be a parent-child relationship, based on photographs, or on famous people.

Notes

This activity combines fluency and accuracy. Because the emphasis is on speed, fluency is a priority for questioners, but because the interviewees get a chance to listen first, they can focus on accuracy.

Activity 71

Don't Say *Yes*

Level	Elementary onwards
Aims	Energiser; practising *Yes/No* questions, short answers and auxiliaries
Duration	10 minutes
Materials	None
Preparation	None

Procedure

1. Demonstrate first yourself. Ask a volunteer to answer your questions. The rule is not to say *Yes* or *No*. Give help where needed.

2. Arrange the students in pairs.

3. They practise asking each other.

4. Invite some students to demonstrate in front of the class.

5. Organise a competition to see how long a student can survive, without saying *Yes* or *No*. Rotate the questioners, as much as possible.

Variation

In another version of this activity, *Yes* is allowed but *No* is not.

Notes

1. It is important to resist the temptation to be the questioner yourself.

2. This activity is good accuracy and fluency practice for the students.

Activity 72

The Class Car

Level	Elementary onwards
Aims	Practising vocabulary
Duration	10 minutes
Materials	Blank paper cut into slips
Preparation	None

Procedure

1. Brainstorm the parts of a car.
2. Ask the students to write one part of a car on each slip of paper.
3. Collect in the slips, shuffle them and give one to each student.
4. The students now have to get up and position themselves, so as to make a car between the whole class.
5. Break the car up, redistribute the slips of paper and repeat the activity.
6. After breaking it up, ask the students to say what they were, where they were, who they were near, and what their function was.
7. Make the car up again and pretend that someone gets in, starts it and drives off. The students act out the journey.

Variations

1. In a large class, they might make two cars.
2. Other possibilities include a bicycle, a face, the human body, etc.

Notes

In order to make the car, they need to ask each other which part they are. Make sure this is done in English and without looking at each other's slips of paper.

Activity 73

The Number Face

Level	Beginners onwards (This activity works particularly well with young learners.)
Aims	Practising numbers and face vocabulary
Duration	10 minutes
Materials	Blank paper
Preparation	Zero

Procedure

1. Elicit the numbers from one to eight. As you do so, write them on the board in such a way that they form a picture of a face in profile, looking left:
   1 = *forehead*, 2 = *eye*, 3 = *ear*, 4 = *nose*, 5 = *mouth*, 6 = *chin*, 7 (drawn twice) = *neck*, 8 (drawn many times) = *hair*
2. Elicit the face vocabulary, calling out the numbers, eg. *'What's 2?' 'Eye!'*, etc.
3. Continue until the students can say the face vocabulary as you point to it.
4. Now practise arithmetic, using only face vocabulary. Give the sum and elicit the answer. For example:
   eye + *ear* = *mouth* (because 2 + 3 = 5)
   hair - *forehead* = *neck*
   eye x *nose* = *hair*
5. Invite the students to make up their own sums.

Variations

1. There is no end to the associations you could make, eg. fruit and vegetables can be drawn, to make up the human body.
2. Instead of arithmetic, surreal stories can be made up, eg. visiting the doctor:
   I was walking down the road when my lettuce started to hurt. I went to the doctor and he took my orange, examined my strawberries and looked into my leek.

Notes

Mismatch is useful for memory association, but the original vocabulary must be understood first.

Activity 74

House of Rods

Level	Beginner onwards
Aims	Practising the vocabulary of buildings and their contents; *there is/are*; prepositions
Duration	20 minutes
Materials	One set of Cuisenaire rods per 8 students (see Variation)
Preparation	None

Procedure

1. Describe a building you know well. Demonstrate in front of the class, using the rods to represent features such as walls, doors, furniture.
2. When you have finished, elicit the features from the class, to check recall.
3. Form pairs or small groups and give out a selection of rods.
4. Ask the students in turn to describe their own houses, or buildings they know well, to their partners.
5. To reinforce the information, ask the listeners to describe the building they have just heard about, either to you or to the whole class, using the rods.

Variations

If you can't get hold of Cuisenaire rods, you can improvise with stationery, pencils, rubbers, etc., or you can just draw pictures.

Notes

1. Cuisenaire rods are small wooden or plastic rods in different colours and lengths. Invented by Cuisenaire for mathematical purposes, they have great potential in the language class. They aid memory association, and so are good for teaching vocabulary, for example.
2. Types of buildings can include the following: house, flat, theatre, cinema, hospital, school, station, airport, shop, etc.

Activity 75

Show us Round!

Level	Elementary onwards
Aims	Practising vocabulary
Duration	10 minutes
Materials	None (but you do need plenty of space!)
Preparation	None

Procedure

1. Demonstrate first yourself. Mime walking through your front door. You are showing someone round your house, saying what you would normally say in such a situation, and pointing to imaginary furniture, etc.
2. Divide the class into pairs and ask the students to show each other round their houses.
3. They describe the house they have just heard about to the rest of the class.
4. The student whose house it is monitors the description for inaccuracies.

Variations

1. Students can show each other round virtually anywhere, eg. their workplace, city, local airport, etc.
2. You can check comprehension by asking the students to draw the house, although it is speaking that obviously provides more language practice.

Notes

1. Encourage the students to go into detail, as this will recycle more language.
2. The students who play the guest can ask as many questions as they like.

Activity 76

Happy Families

Level	Elementary onwards
Aims	Practising *have got* and vocabulary
Duration	20 minutes
Materials	Four pictures per student or pair of students (see Note 1)
Preparation	None (if you have the pictures ready)

Procedure

1. Divide the class into groups of four students and give each group 16 pictures.
2. Ask them to put the pictures into four sets of four, using any system they like.
3. It is useful later if they write out lists of words in the sets they have chosen.
4. Ask a student in each group to shuffle all the pictures and deal them out like playing cards. Each student gets four cards.
5. The aim is to collect four pictures which belong to the same set.
6. This is done by the students in turn asking another student *'Have you got ...?'* and naming the picture they want.
7. If the second student has that picture, they exchange. If not, nothing is exchanged, and the turn is over. Everyone should always have four cards.
8. The winner is the first student to collect a full set of four pictures.

Variations

1. You can vary the size of groups and picture sets.
2. You can have extra cards and deal out a hidden 'dummy' hand, which does not come into play, thereby frustrating some players.

Notes

1. The pictures can be cut from magazines, etc., and can be of any vocabulary you want to revise, although the best suited are words that collocate with *'Have you got ...?'*, eg. possessions, objects, family, animals, shopping items, illnesses/injuries, etc.
2. You can enlist the help of students to collect pictures, and build up the collection slowly. Once you have them, keep them for future use.
3. It is much better if the students group the pictures themselves, as it leads to more recycling and discussion.

Activity 77

I Have Never

Level	Elementary onwards
Aims	Practising the present perfect to express experiences
Duration	10 minutes
Materials	Blank paper
Preparation	None

Procedure

1. Ask the students to think of five things they have never done.
2. They write five sentences, starting *I have never ...,* on separate slips of paper.
3. Collect these slips, mix them up and put them on a chair or in a bag or box.
4. Each student in turn picks one of the slips.
5. They read the sentence aloud and then have to say who they think wrote it, and why (see Variation 1).
6. They ask that person the corresponding question, eg. *'Have you ever ...?'*, and receive an appropriate reply.
7. If the answer is *No,* they ask the same person if they wrote the sentence.

Variations

1. It is fun to do this in teams, as it puts more pressure and more interest on guessing the original writer correctly.
2. Each student can pick one slip and find out who wrote it by asking as many students as necessary, then report back to the class.
3. It is natural to extend the conversation to include *Would you like to ...?* and *What was it like?*

Notes

Make sure the students write legibly.

Activity 78

Photo Postures

Level	Elementary onwards
Aims	Practising imperatives and the vocabulary of the body
Duration	10 minutes
Materials	Photos of people in interesting poses
Preparation	None (if you already have the photos)

Procedure

1. Revise imperatives and brainstorm body vocabulary with the class.
2. Arrange the students in pairs.
3. Give one student a photo. The other mustn't see it. Demonstrate the activity first yourself, if necessary.
4. The first student must give their partner instructions, in order to make the same pose as that of the photo. No hand gestures are allowed.
5. Allow the rest of the class see the finished postures.
6. Exchange the roles.

Variation

Photos of couples can be used for groups of four students.

Notes

This is an amusing, energising activity. It is fun to finish off by giving photos of impossible poses, such as complicated yoga positions.

Activity 79
Animal Logic

Level	Beginner onwards
Aims	Practising the present simple
Duration	10-15 minutes
Materials	Copies of the task opposite
Preparation	2 minutes

Procedure

1. Give out copies of the task opposite to students, in pairs or in groups.
2. Ask them to work together to solve the puzzle.
3. Invite them to justify their answers.
4. Challenge the students to design their own puzzles.
5. Distribute these and repeat the activity as above.

Variations

1. Different groups can design different activities.
2. If the students design their own puzzles, you can keep them for another lesson, too.

Notes

1. Lots of puzzles lend themselves to this kind of activity.
2. You may need to help some students with the method. It is a good idea to draw a table, and also to note down negative information as well as positive. The clues must be read twice, as earlier clues can relate to later information.
3. Passive knowledge of the present simple is needed to read the clues, but active knowledge is required to speak about the puzzle and to design another.

Key

Alfie:	monkey	reads	smokes
Butch:	dog	opera	whisky
Charlie:	lion	stamps	rock
Dennis:	bull	golf	disco

DESIGNED TO PHOTOCOPY

Animal Logic

There are four animals: Alfie, Butch, Charlie and Dennis, and they each have two hobbies.

The lion doesn't like golf very much.

Alfie hates golf but reads a newspaper.

Charlie isn't a bull.

Charlie collects stamps but the monkey doesn't.

Alfie isn't a lion.

The dog drinks whisky but never plays golf.

Butch isn't a bull.

The lion, who collects stamps, doesn't go to the opera.

Charlie is a rock singer, but he never smokes a pipe.

The monkey doesn't like whisky, stamp collecting or golf.

The bull can't read.

The monkey's name starts with the first letter of the alphabet.

Dennis often plays golf and the bull enjoys disco dancing.

Butch enjoys listening to opera music.

Who is the lion, the bull, the dog and the monkey, and what are their hobbies?

Activity 80
Drama Dialogues

Level	Elementary onwards
Aims	Practising dialogues; speaking practice
Duration	15 minutes
Materials	None
Preparation	None

Procedure

1. Select a dialogue and write it on the board or OHP (see Note 2).
2. Make sure the students understand it, and drill where appropriate.
3. Ask them to practise the dialogue in pairs or small groups (depending on the number of parts there are).
4. Ask them to practise saying the dialogue in role and in situation, with actions, eg. normal, serious, happy, as old people, on the moon, as cowboys, as horses, as children, in the disco.
5. Allow the students to suggest new situations.

Notes

1. Don't force anyone to act if they don't want to. Get to know your class before attempting this kind of activity, and warm up to it with other games, if necessary.
2. I remember a dialogue that worked very well:

    A: *Hi, what are you doing?*
    B: *I'm cooking eggs.*
    A: *Can I try some?*
    B: *Sure.*
    A: *Ugh, these are awful. I think I'm going to die!*
    B: *Oh no! He's dying. I'll get a doctor.*
    Doctor: *I'm sorry. He's dead.*

Activity 81
Circle Story

Level	Elementary onwards
Aims	Practising speaking and listening to others
Duration	15 minutes
Materials	A very short story (see page 89), cut into about 10 sentences, for each group of students
Preparation	2 minutes

Procedure

1. Arrange the students into a circle (in a large class make several circles of about ten students).
2. Give each circle the whole story, so that each student gets one sentence.
3. They mustn't show their sentences to anyone. Instead, they should read them out to each other.
4. Their task is twofold: to put the story in order and to sit in the correct order.
5. When they have finished, they read out the whole story.
6. Discuss the meaning or message of the story.

Variation

The activity can be done without having to change places and get in order. The students can still put the story in order.

Notes

1. Some process language might be introduced early on. They might need certain expressions, eg. *You go before me, My part is next, I'm between him and her,* etc.
2. It doesn't matter if each student is given more than one sentence. They will just have to occupy two chairs, and hop from one to the other.
3. Putting stories in order involves a lot of language analysis and attention to detail.
4. A good story always leaves scope for discussion afterwards.

DESIGNED TO PHOTOCOPY

A Circle Story Story

The Difference between Penzance and John O'Groats

A man sat on a rock by a stream enjoying the peace of the moment.

A traveller came by and asked him the way to John O'Groats and what it was like.

'Where are you from?' asked the man on the rock. 'Penzance,' replied the traveller.

'And what's Penzance like?' asked the man.

'Oh, it's a shocking place, depressing, unfriendly and dangerous,' came the answer.

'Oh dear. Well, you'll probably find John O'Groats much the same,' concluded the man on the rock.

An hour later another traveller from Penzance came by, asking exactly the same questions.

'And what's Penzance like?' asked the man for the second time that day.

'Oh, it's a wonderful place, so inspiring, friendly, clean and safe.'

'How nice. Then you'll probably find John O'Groats much the same,' concluded the man on the rock by the stream.

Activity 82

Used to Jokes

Level	Intermediate onwards
Aims	Practising *used to* for past habits and states; practising giving explanations
Duration	15 minutes
Materials	A copy or copies of the jokes below, or an OHP transparency
Preparation	2 minutes (to photocopy the jokes, write them on the board, or prepare the transparency)

Procedure

1. Show the jokes to the students. Point out that they are not in order.
2. Ask them to put them in order and check their answers.
3. Whether the students find them funny or not, ask how the jokes work.
4. Demonstrate an explanation of the first joke:
   'It implies that he was arrogant in the past, and this was bad, but that he isn't now, because now there's nothing wrong with him, but of course he still is conceited by saying he's perfect.'
5. Ask the students to practise explaining the jokes to each other.
6. Invite them to explain the jokes to the whole class.
7. Ask if there are any jokes of this type in their own language. If there are, ask if they can be translated and, if so, encourage the students to share them.

Variation

You can suggest they investigate jokes in their own language for homework.

Notes

1. Remember that photocopying makes students lazy! Get them to read the jokes and copy them by hand if possible.
2. Help with vocabulary where necessary.
3. Humour often brightens proceedings, but it can be embarrassing if students don't appreciate or understand the joke. Explain that the jokes may not be funny at all, but that these in particular are excellent examples of this structure.
4. The vocabulary can be simplified, eg. 1 *I used to feel superior ...* .

Key

1e) 2g) 3b) 4c) 5f) 6a) 7d)

DESIGNED TO PHOTOCOPY

Used to Jokes

Match these sentence halves to make jokes:

1 I used to be conceited	a) but now I'm not so sure ...
2 I never used to finish anything,	b) but now I'm in two minds about it.
3 I used to be schizophrenic	c) but I'm all right noOOOOOoow ...!
4 I used to be a werewolf	d) but noww I donnt haavv enny rrobblemmz.
5 I never used to be a vegetarian	e) but now I'm perfect.
6 I used to be indecisive	f) but now I always have vegetables with my meat.
7 I used to be unable to spell	g) but now I ...

Activity 83

Lateral Thinking

Level	Intermediate onwards
Aims	Practising *Yes/No* questions
Duration	5 minutes per puzzle
Materials	A copy of the *Lateral Thinking Puzzles* (see page 92) cut up into individual puzzles
Preparation	1 minute (to copy the puzzles)

Procedure

1. Give a demonstration of the activity. Tell the class a puzzle and invite the students to ask you the reasons behind it by means of *Yes/No* questions. You can only say *Yes* or *No* in response to their questions. Keep going until they find the solution.

2. Give out the other puzzles to some students. It doesn't matter if the majority don't get one, as they will be the ones working on the solution.

3. Ask each student to come out and read the puzzle to the class, who ask questions until they solve it.

4. Time the activity. The student with the puzzle that lasts longest is the winner.

Variation

You don't have to do all the puzzles in the same lesson. You can have one every day.

Notes

These puzzles are not new, but often it is the teacher who sets a problem and answers the questions. This is tiring and demands your full attention. If the students assume that role, they practise more language, freeing you to monitor the language and the class dynamics.

DESIGNED TO PHOTOCOPY

Lateral Thinking Puzzles

1 There's a dead man lying in a field. What happened?

Answer: *He was wearing a parachute which didn't open. He fell into the field.*

2 Anthony and Cleopatra lie dead on the living room floor. There's water and broken glass on the floor. How did they die?

Answer: *They were goldfish in a tank, knocked over by a dog.*

3 A man walked into a bar and ordered a glass of water. Instead, the barman pulled a gun on him, but the man said 'Thanks' and left the bar satisfied. Why?

Answer: *He'd had hiccoughs, which are curable by drinking water or by a sudden shock.*

4 Two pieces of coal and a carrot are lying together in a field. Why?

Answer: *They were on a snowman's face. The snowman melted.*

5 A man is found dead, hanging by the neck from the ceiling of an empty factory warehouse. There is no chair he could have jumped off. There's water on the floor. How did he manage to hang himself?

Answer: *It is a hot climate and the factory produces ice. He stood on a block of ice until it melted.*

6 A woman is woken up by the phone, but the caller hangs up, satisfied. Why?

Answer: *The caller is next door and couldn't sleep because of the woman's snoring. The phone call interrupted the snoring.*

7 A man passes a window, hears the phone ringing and screams. Why?

Answer: *He'd decided to commit suicide by jumping out of a skyscraper window, because after a nuclear war he thought he was the last person left alive. The phone ringing disproves that, but it's too late, as he's already falling through the air.*

8 A man makes a return journey by train to see his doctor, but on the way back commits suicide. Why?

Answer: *He'd gone for an operation to cure his blindness. On the way home the train went through a tunnel, and the man thought his blindness had returned.*

Activity 84

Song Antonyms

Level	Elementary onwards
Aims	Practising vocabulary; listening
Duration	15-20 minutes
Materials	A song on cassette; blank paper
Preparation	5 minutes

Procedure

1. Before class, study or recall the lyrics to a song. Choose some key words and think of approximate antonyms (opposites) for these words.
2. Write them in a vertical list on the board.
3. Arrange the class into teams, either pairs or small groups.
4. Each team writes down one antonym for every word in the list on the board.
5. Tell them that they will hear something on the cassette. They get one point every time their words are mentioned, including all repetitions.
6. Count up the points to see who the winners are.
7. Elicit which words appeared in the song, pairing them with your list of opposites on the board.
8. Elicit as much of the song as you can.

Variations

1. You can vary the antonyms, and the number of them, according to the students' level.
2. You can vary the number of opposites for each word, eg. *light* has *dark, gloomy, heavy,* etc., according to level and time.
3. You might ask the students to put the words in the order that they appear in the song.

Notes

It is not necessary to have a copy of the lyrics for this activity. The song should be clear and preferably well-known. I always use *Yesterday* by The Beatles, and my list of antonyms includes *tomorrow, near, there, gradually, woman, light, come, right, short, hate, work, show.*

Activity 85

Wordbuilding to Music

Level	Elementary onwards
Aims	Practising listening; wordbuilding
Duration	15 minutes
Materials	Blank paper
Preparation	It depends how well you know the song you choose.

Procedure

1. Choose a song which is fairly rich in vocabulary, eg. nouns, verbs, adjectives and adverbs.
2. Ask the students to draw a table of four columns and to label them *Nouns, Verbs, Adjectives* and *Adverbs.*
3. Dictate some of the key words in the song, but change the part of speech, eg. if it says *beautiful* in the song, dictate *beauty* or *beautifully.*
4. The students have to write the word in the correct column.
5. Group the students, so that they can compare and help each other. They then complete all the gaps in the grid, using dictionaries if they like.
6. Go over the answers, not forgetting pronunciation, and drill where appropriate.
7. Play the song.
8. The students tick any words they hear, in the appropriate column according to the part of speech.
9. Ask the students to try to remember the line in which their words appeared.
10. They listen to the song again and again, until they can reconstruct the lyrics.

Variation

You can vary the number of words in the table, and also the number of parts of speech, eg. you might wish to include opposites of adjectives and adverbs, using prefixes.

Notes

It is not necessary to have a copy of the lyrics for this activity. The song should be clear and preferably well-known. I always use *The Logical Song* by Supertramp.

Activity 86

Ring of Words

Level	Elementary onwards
Aims	Practising vocabulary, writing and listening
Duration	25 minutes
Materials	Blank paper
Preparation	None

Procedure

1. Give the students eight or ten key words from a song you know. Write them in random order in a ring on the board, and ask them to copy them down.
2. Individually, in pairs or in small groups, ask the students to make up a short story using all the words.
3. Invite them to tell their stories to the class.
4. Play the song. Ask the students to tick the words as they hear them, and at the same time put them in order.
5. In pairs, they try to remember the lines in which they heard the words.
6. Challenge them to reconstruct the whole song if appropriate. Play the song for them again as necessary.

Variation

The students can predict what the song is about from the ring of words, before writing their own stories.

Notes

1. It is not necessary to have a copy of the lyrics for this activity. The song should be clear and preferably well-known. I always use *Norwegian Wood* by The Beatles, and the ring of words includes *girl, room, anywhere, chair, wine, morning, wood, laugh, bird, fire.*

Activity 87

Collaborative Story Dictation

Level	Elementary onwards
Aims	Practising the four skills
Duration	20 minutes
Materials	Blank paper; the story (see page 95)
Preparation	None

Procedure

1. Divide the class into four groups.
2. Dictate five different sentences to each group, in random order.
3. Ask the students to write each sentence on a separate slip of paper. Make sure each student writes all five sentences.
4. When they have finished, allow some time for conferring.
5. Re-arrange the class so that every new group has at least one student from each of the old groups. You need as many new groups as there were students in the smallest old group.
6. The new groups have all 20 sentences. They have to put them in the correct order.

Variation

For heterogeneous classes, you can select longer sentences for the stronger groups (without making it obvious).

Notes

1. Organise the sentences beforehand and number them.
2. The students can ask for repetitions, if necessary.

DESIGNED TO PHOTOCOPY

Peter and Lucy

Once upon a time there were two lovers, called Peter and Lucy,

who lived either side of a dangerous river.

They saw each other secretly every day.

Peter, who had a boat, always visited Lucy, usually in the evenings after work.

One day, Lucy was a little surprised that Peter didn't turn up.

After three days, she was worried that something bad had happened to Peter.

So she decided to go and find him.

First she asked Michael, the boatbuilder, to take her across the river.

But Michael wanted to charge her, and she had no money.

She asked Stephen, who had a boat, to help her,

but he said he would only take her if she slept with him.

She went back and told her parents everything, and asked them for some money.

Michael took her across, but refused to wait for her.

When she eventually found Peter's house, another woman answered the door.

She tried to see Peter, but in vain.

Heartbroken, she wandered around for a while, then thought about getting back home.

There was no boat, so she walked two miles to a bridge,

which was guarded by a soldier called Oscar.

He stopped her, saying that his General had forbidden anyone to cross the bridge.

In the end, she swam into the dangerous river and died.

Epilogue

This book has attempted to achieve a workable combination of efficient strategies. Some of these aim to conserve or exploit inputs to make them longer-lasting or more versatile. Others aim to activate the students into producing more output and to promote more effective learning. Most of the strategies, however, aim to do both at the same time.

Perhaps now is a good time to reacquaint ourselves with the eleven fictitious, beleaguered teachers we met in the Introduction. Why they are under so much stress may now be somewhat clearer:

John and **Mary** might benefit from minimising their input, giving the students more responsibility and thinking about using student-generated and personalised activities.

Jane will remind her students how much more they will learn by doing the above.

Adam would benefit from the above ideas, and also from making the most of his prepared materials: adapting the level, adopting a flexible approach and encouraging a greater degree of autonomy in his learners.

Jack might be better off preparing less elaborate materials and even involving the students in collecting them for him.

Roy should keep his materials filed, ready for use.

Helen might find the debates will work on their own, allowing the students to express what they really think.

Sally could take a less central role and challenge the students with tasks and roles of responsibility, giving them a touch of the limelight, too, while allowing herself the chance to evaluate their performance.

Pete could also involve and challenge his adolescents more, so that they are not so passive, and this may be enough to avoid negativity.

Judith could ask the students to check and redraft work before she sees it, so that the marking is reduced, and she might also benefit from not giving numerical marks, so that they read her comments and learn from her advice.

Mark would find life easier with a simple filing system of labelled binders and folders, set up at the start of term and kept in order throughout the year. A little effort at the right time can save hours of stress and turmoil later on.

All of these considerations are based on the ten MINIMAX Principles (pages 10-11), which have served as the pedagogical foundation of this book.